The Road to Somewhere
An American Memoir
James A. Reeves

W. W. Norton & Company
New York | London

The Road to Somewhere: An American Memoir
Copyright © 2011 by James A. Reeves
james@bigamericannight.com
www.bigamericannight.com

Book design and composition by James A. Reeves
Manufactured by South China Printing Co. Ltd.

Library of Congress Cataloging-in-Publication Data
Reeves, James A.
The road to somewhere : an American memoir / by James A. Reeves. -- 1st ed.
p. cm.
Includes index.
ISBN 978-0-393-34005-1 (pbk.)
1. United States--Description and travel. 2. United States--Pictorial works. 3. Reeves,
James A.--Travel--United States. 4. Men--Travel--United States. 5. Masculinity--United
States. 6. United States--Social life and customs--1971- 7. United States--Social
conditions--1980- 8. National characteristics, American. I. Title.
E169.Z83R43 2011
973.92--dc22
2010044400

W. W. Norton & Company
500 Fifth Avenue, New York, NY 10110
www.wwnorton.com

W. W. Norton & Company Ltd.
Castle House, 75/76 Wells Street, London, WIT 3QT

1 2 3 4 5 6 7 8 9 0

This book is dedicated to my mom, who told me to go out into the world and look around. I miss you.

I am an American. I say this to myself and marvel at the tangled reaction. There is the flush of embarrassment, the red tingling of some humiliation or slight that I cannot recall; I feel as though I owe somebody an apology. There is the apprehension that comes with knowing I am sheltered, a sense of being fattened up to be set loose among the hunters, the fierce entitlement of an only child. As for the pride and strength that are so often sung about these days, there is some of that; it is a small yet undeniable core that is muffled by the red faced and jittery feelings, the sense of being foolish, of being misrepresented. Of being unprepared.

Men

This is a story about being a man in America.

More specifically, it's about me being a man in America.
Or trying.

Of course it's about my father. This type of book is
always about sons and fathers.

And his father.

And this guy sitting on a bench: my grandfather's grandfather. Daddy Reeves, they called him. Born in 1849 in a Canadian forest. Some say he was adopted. Others say his parents couldn't afford to keep him. As a teenager, he worked as a fur trader for the Hudson Bay Company. He got married and had a daughter and a son. After losing his wife and daughter a few years later, he wandered into Michigan and built a perch fishery on Saginaw Bay where Lake Huron swoops down to form lower Michigan's iconic mitten. He bought the land for $750 and there he settled, remarrying and raising his son and five daughters. Nobody knows much about what he left behind in Canada.

But everybody knows about that bench. After closing the fishery each night, he would walk two miles to the bar in Caseville, where he served as postmaster general. As the years passed, the walk began to tire him out. In 1908, he talked to the mayor and the town installed a bench at the halfway point between his fishery and the bar, where he would stop each evening to rest and read the day's paper.

This photograph is as close as I can come to explaining why I am an American.

What does it mean to be a man? Here's a photograph that I found stuck to the bottom of a forgotten box deep in the back of my parents' attic: it's a party circa 1960, back when wood-paneled recreation rooms were the place to be. The man gestures broadly with a cigarette as he leans into a woman who doesn't look too happy about it. Nobody knows who he is. But he knows who he is. You can tell.

Road Trip. In 1941, my grandfather drove across the country from Detroit to California to deliver a car and see the World's Fair in San Francisco. There were no highways, the car broke down constantly, he slept in fields, and he said it was the best trip of his life. He hitchhiked home. Three years later he landed in France in World War II. Marched through France and into Germany. "Patton was right," my grandfather told me. "We should have gone after Stalin when we had the chance."

After the war, he got married in his uniform, finished a business degree at the University of Michigan, and took a job at Sears, where he would work for 38 years until his retirement in 1982. He moved into a house where the family fishery once stood and he served as township commissioner of Caseville, where he knew everybody by name.

My father followed in his footsteps. Except the war was Vietnam and Sears started offshoring its manufacturing. My dad changed after he lost his job, moving among various retail positions and the occasional pyramid scheme, and keeping to himself, hardly speaking at all.

And me? I spent a summer working the cash register in the lighting department at Sears, but I've had twenty-eight jobs since I started working at fifteen, ranging from the night shift at a gas station to selling oriental rugs to teaching graduate school to running a graphic design studio. I've never gone to war and I've never been punched. My life in New York City feels insulated, detached from responsibility, and the effect is compounded by the fact that most of my activities are conducted in front of a computer screen.

I am a million miles away from my father and grandfather, who played by a different set of rules: a belief in country and companies, a dogged faith in firm handshakes and settling down.

I decide to go for a drive. And I keep driving, thinking I might learn a thing or two. New Jersey, Arizona, Pennsylvania, Indiana, Kansas. Whenever I can find some time and a cheap rental car, I pack a bag and drive. Oklahoma, Wyoming, California, Tennessee, Oregon, North Carolina. Sometimes I'll point the car toward the ocean, other times I'll pick an interesting city or a small town along the border. Florida, Texas, Montana, New Mexico, Delaware, and North Dakota.

I keep driving, thinking that I might figure out what I'm made of, that I might discover what it means to be a man in America.

AM Radio Scan. "It's when you connect all of them, it's when you look at all of the different dots, that's when you see the picture and I can see the picture that it's making: they are building a machine and it's something that you don't want them to turn on."

I flip through the stations and a woman says that temper tantrums are expensive ways of problem solving. I switch back: "And what will turn on this machine? An event. I don't know what that event is, but God help us, we must stand together. We must stand strong. An emergency will turn the machine on and once you turn the machine on, there's no turning back. You must not give them more power. You must not!"

Turn the dial and a preacher booms: "Do you think Jesus never felt desire for a woman? He was tempted! But he resisted temptation because he did not want to lose his identity, lose his effectiveness, and lose his destiny. Temptation is everywhere you turn! You turn on the computer and —"

Change the station.

"— and unfortunately, he caught the attention of the government."

"Uh oh."

"Right. And remember, we're talking about a small mountain town. University of Tennessee football is the biggest thing in the state, okay? And nobody in Knoxville can stop them from firing an automatic—"

I flip to a baseball game on the radio. I don't like baseball and I have no idea what the announcers are talking about, but their drowsy murmur is comforting and I listen for several innings until I find a cheap motel.

Country

What does it mean to be a man? A man has politics. He knows where he stands. He takes charge. He's authentic and genuine. An original. I've learned these things from commercials.

Driving down a miracle mile, I see whiskey advertisements telling me that I'm a class act. A billboard for beer promises an exciting night. A deodorant company offers an embarrassing orgy. An advertisement for a pair of khakis says that I need to be more rugged. Another poster tells me that I'm missing out on the excitement. The one next to it says that I don't need to fit in. Every single piece of printed material is telling me that I'm a disaster.

A real man ignores these messages. He's busy making decisions. He's breaking hearts and fixing things.

Message. There's a big electric sign just before the Delaware Bridge on southbound I-95 that says *If You Are in Crisis, Call 1-800-273-TALK*. I often think about this sign as I fall asleep, how right now it's blinking somewhere out there in the big American night. I imagine all the different people zooming under it at eighty miles per hour and I wonder what kind of person might dial that number. Will I ever call?

Gas City. Leave the politics, guns, and sprawl aside: America frightens me on purely geographical terms. So many blank spaces on the map, all of these shocking white rectangles where God knows what's happening. I want to drive up to the edge and take a look. I rent a Chrysler and fantasize about the romance of the open road: the coming-of-age stories paired with exit signs and motor lodges, the road trip as mythologized in an endless library of songs, books, and movies. Do other countries hold such passion for their highways?

Welcome to Indiana, the self-declared crossroads of America. Windows down, music roaring, driving hard. I speed through a town called Gas City. Sometimes I listen to talk radio. *If we look around today, just as the Scripture says, the prophetic clouds are gathering . . .* I try to imagine what it would feel like to believe in Jesus.

There are so many beached cars along the corridors of the interstate: are these acts of desperation or simply the result of some sunburnt jackass trying to shave a few minutes off his estimated arrival? I dare myself to shut my eyes while going ninety. I do it three times, ten seconds each. I promise to stop. Do it any longer and it'll become a compulsion. Can't crack up on the first day.

Some things just stick with you. Grotesque trivia: *the largest and heaviest organ is the skin*. Or melancholy phrases: *he died alone in Tunisia*. These bits remain fresh in the mind long after their roots have faded away; they appear at the edges of sleep, odd and tantalizing references, which the mind scours for details: *berserkers painted themselves black and gnawed at their shields*.

Strange fragments churn up when you're barreling down the highway after midnight, dazzled by the lights of cities you cannot identify. Sometimes you catch big authoritative thoughts that feel like they might hold everything together, if only for a moment: *capitalism thrives on inequality*. Sometimes your mental chatter kicks up a few brilliant ideas that you just don't have the time to make happen: *a reality show called "Who's Going to Cry First?"* Or the first line for a terrific novel that you will never write: *A damning journal is found, read aloud to the world, and our hero is exposed*.

These disjointed ideas smash together before the next cluster of neon lights snaps your attention back to the road, and it is difficult to tell if writing them down for others is instructive or annoying.

Weekender. Sometimes I'll grab a car and tear off on the first road I can find, not caring about the direction. Doesn't matter. Things will sort themselves out and the trip will develop its own story line and that's the best part. Get on those weird dirt roads with serious geography, those dark back channels where either you say "How's it goin'?" and nod when you pass somebody or you eye each other suspiciously.

I fly to Kansas City on a Friday night and twenty minutes later I'm racing along the Missouri River, weaving in and out of Kansas, Missouri, Iowa, and Nebraska. I have no idea what state I'm in when I crash into a motel and fall asleep to motorcycle engines gunning in the parking lot and the treble-twang of country music from the dead-ender bar up the road. In the morning I pull back the curtain on nothing but big cornfields and heavy silence. In search of provisions, I head to the nearest town but all of the shops are closed or abandoned, so I buy everything I need at a Wal-Mart, which rises like a temple in the middle of the flat green. A charger for my phone, deodorant, toothpaste, nail clippers, cigarettes, socks.

Nebraska is tougher than I expected. There's a shocking amount of corn and sky and empty space that oscillates between tranquil and unsettling; driving alongside the tracks of the old Union Pacific route takes me past alien farming structures, scrapyards, federal agriculture research stations, and small towns where twitchy gangbangers in red bandannas stand in the median, leaning against low-slung cars with custom paint jobs and flashing neck tattoos and studs all over their faces. A dog runs up to my window, foam dripping from its jaws.

I screech to a stop in Longpole, Wyoming, nearly wrapping my car around ten or twelve Hell's Angels hoisting beer bottles and shouting in the middle of the road while waving a big American flag. Citizens gather in a church parking lot to watch the ruckus, a few cheering them on while others scowl. An old woman walks over to them, salutes their flag, and marches back to her yard.

Nearly all of the men wear cowboy hats in Cheyenne. They tuck their thumbs into wide belts with big silver buckles that hide beneath serious guts. They drink bottles of Michelob and some of them howl at a country band playing beneath a tent in the park next to Interstate 80. I feel alien, trying to find my footing and make some small talk. These are the Frontier Days, a weeklong celebration of Cheyenne's former reputation as "Hell on Wheels," a lawless outpost for gambling and thieving, now a tourist destination with annual reenactments.

Drive Alone. Sometimes it's all about watching the numbers run: the miles clicking by, the dollars and cents on the gas pump, the feverish mental math as you calculate ambitious arrival times. Other times the odometer fades away and you just drive and listen to your mind chatter. So many things crash your senses while racing down the road: billboards, church signs, memorials to car wreck victims, sinister factories blowing fire into the night. All of it is important, all of it seems full of secret meaning. Clues to something personal or national, it's hard to say, but the bus depots, shabby motels, title pawn shops, penitentiaries, and blinking neon feel like pieces to a grand puzzle that will shatter as soon as you cut the ignition.

Point the car in any direction and go it alone until that back road you've been riding for a hundred and eighty-six miles hits a dead end and it's time to decide: Nashville or Little Rock? Get out of the car, listen to the insects thrum in the summer dark, and think it over. This is how you drive America.

Time and distance get strange after a few days on the road and driving becomes the means and the end. The beautiful simplicity of moving from point A to point B. I could do this forever, driving from town to town, looking at things.

Highway 12. I pull into a dark trucker motel next to a Christian Supply store. The manager doesn't wear a shirt and his belly sits on the counter next to my room key and credit card. He's watching the History Channel and smoking Marlboro Menthol 100s. Motels are always dramatic. Even without the crooked lampshades, stained carpets, and dead air there is always something melancholy inside these rooms. Maybe it's the weather of strangers. Maybe it comes from the movies. The manager imprints my credit card and shoves the key under the bulletproof glass. "Checkout's at ten sharp."

I fumble with the lock and shoulder open the door. There's a wood-paneled Zenith mounted on the wall, cigarette burns on the bedspread, and somebody kicked in the air conditioner and stole the telephone.

Origin Story. I remember my father coming home with his briefcase and sitting on the kitchen counter with a beer while "Leaving on a Jet Plane" played in the other room and my mom cooked beef stroganoff. I would play around on the linoleum with my trucks or the dog while he talked about his day, and I remember my parents being very happy.

Before I was born, my parents drove from Chicago to Denver. This was a few weeks after a doctor told my mom that she would never be able to get pregnant. But she was sick all the way through Nebraska and all the way back through the Dakotas and Wisconsin. Turns out she could get pregnant, after all.

Woman in the Road. I'm ripping through the Smoky Mountains late on a Tuesday night, driving fast and hard on some chewed-up back road, corkscrewing up and down the side of phantom geography. The mountains are heavy shadows against the blue-black night and sometimes the trees get tangled over the road, branches slapping and scraping the windshield. Two in the morning and I'm racing through one of these tree tunnels, the only car for hours. My headlights are the only thing around and they flash on something long-legged and fast-running with big eyes: a shocked woman in a negligee scrambling to the shoulder of the road. She's a half mile in my rearview by the time this image registers and two more miles pass before I find a place to turn around that won't send me over the edge.

I must turn around, even though she will sweetly ask for a ride and then slit my throat. Or a man will burst from the bushes, pointing his gun sideways and yelling like a punk. I've seen enough movies to know that getting involved with a young woman on the side of a lonesome road always leads to trouble. But I won't be able to sleep knowing that I left someone in the middle of the mountains.

My headlights catch her in the middle of the road, mouth wide open. I brake and turn off the radio. She's clutching a cat to her chest and staring at me, shifting from foot to foot.

"You okay?"

She nods.

"You sure?"

"I'm fine. Just needed the walk."

She looks annoyed. I don't ask about the cat. "Well, it's late and this is the middle of nowhere, so I was worried . . ."

"Really, I'm fine. But thank you."

"Okay. I'm going to drive away now."

"Okay."

And I go. I race through the black-green tunnel for another hour until I finally reach a motel and I do not sleep well that night because somewhere there is a spooky young woman in lingerie wandering an obscure mountain road with a house cat, and I'll never know what she was doing out there.

Traffic Jam. Everybody's flying through Pennsylvania, whipping along I-80's dips and curves at ninety miles per hour. My mind buzzes with crazy-person math: *if I maintain an average of eighty-five, I should get to New York around 9:32, which would be forty-seven minutes earlier than if I were going eighty* . . . Around sunset, traffic grinds down near mile marker #282.

We stop. We put it in park. After fifteen minutes, people get out of their cars: a gigantic muscleman with a fantastic Afro in a neon tank top, a small guy covered in tattoos with a silver ponytail under an American flag bandanna, an old lady in a flaming red tracksuit. We stretch, we smoke, we pace. We kick at the gravel and make bad jokes and abuse the word "surreal." Some of us sit on the guardrails and take pictures of the situation with our telephones.

After the sun sets, we turn off our headlights and sit in the dark. A fat man in a tie-dyed shirt jogs past my window and a woman's voice calls out, "This is too far, Larry, I think we should turn back." I quiz the trucker next to me. His cab says Minnesota Rapid Transport and his CB radio squawks with information. We gather at his door to listen: "Yeah guys, we got two rigs all tangled up" — *laughter* — "fuel spill" — "hope you packed something to eat" — *profanity* — "a few Jersey barriers knocked across the bridge." The owner of the Cherokee in front of me marches off into the trees to pee and it's incredibly loud.

Two hours later, those of us with small cars start wiggling back and forth, angling for the shoulder. Everybody cooperates, inching back to give the other guy some room. A man in a t-shirt that says *I Love Hot Moms* gives me a thumbs-up and waves me forward, making sure I don't overshoot the shoulder and land in the valley below. We leave the trucks behind, their owners clustered together and conferring in the highway, their red cigarette tips pulsing in the night. Soon enough we're back to cutting each other off and flashing our high beams, but for a while there we were very well behaved.

You Never Sausage a Place.

The signs never stop:

> *You'll Be Tickled Pink at South of the Border. 90 Miles.*
> *Time for a Paws? South of the Border. 72 Miles.*
> *You Never Sausage a Place! (Everybody's a Weiner at Pedro's!)*
> *Roads' Scholar! 27 miles.*
> *Somtheeng Dee'frent! South of the Border. 26 miles.*
> *Keep Yelling Kids, They'll Stop.*
> *Pedro's Weather Report: Chilly Today, Hot Tamale! 21 miles.*
> *Too Moch Tequila! South of the Border.*

For over 170 miles I-95 delivers a relentless attack of puns from a cartoon bandito named Pedro who desperately urges you to visit South of the Border. Thirty billboards later, you finally reach the state line that separates the Carolinas and of course you're going to stop and find out what the hell Pedro has been banging on about for the past three hours: it's the biggest rest stop/tourist trap/fireworks store/mini-golf compound in the world. With trucker showers.

Pedro wears a sombrero, a poncho, and a silly mustache. He's cute in the fever-dream racist way of a flickering old Disney cartoon, and the effect is compounded when he's 100 feet tall and surrounded by Pedro's Pleasure Dome, Pedro's Reality Ride, and the Sombrero Room Restaurant.

South of the Border started in 1950 as a bar by Alan Schafer, which was a popular oasis from North Carolina's dry counties. According to *Roadside America*, "He began to import Mexican souvenirs, and on one such trip arranged for two Mexican boys to come to America and work for him. As Schafer said, 'Somebody began calling them Pedro and Pancho, and since it fit into the theme, we began calling them both Pedro.' Today, all SOB workers, regardless of race, creed or color, are called Pedro."

I park the car and gaze up at Pedro's dead painted eyes. A couple of college kids holler at the animal statues. Families wander through the parking lot, looking confused as they pass by Pedro's Africa Shop and Pedro's Leather Shop. There are military discounts at the fireworks supermarket. It might be one of the ickiest parts of America, but it's also one of the most brilliantly marketed. I stopped.

Waffle House, Part 1. The South begins somewhere around Rocky Mount, North Carolina. This is where the Starbucks become Waffle Houses. I wake up at the Interstate Inn and smoke a few Pall Malls in bed, but my heart's not in it. I'm sick with the flu, living in a head that feels a million miles under, hacking and sniffling, juiced up on bad caffeine. I stare at my reflection in the broken wood-paneled TV that hangs from a black metal arm, then I undo the chains on the door and step into the hard bright sun. There's a Waffle House across the street. I walk over.

Confession: I feel bad because I drove like a complete ass last night. Riding the left lane the whole way down I-95, burying my bumper in your taillights, flashing my highbeams, knocking you out of the left lane. Get off the road or I will gobble you up. The other drivers looked crazed: dead-eyed and grinning at nothing, or singing along to songs nobody else can hear. From behind my stuffy head, it played out like a video game. Rumble strips and toll booths and no Hazmats. I drove terribly because I have only 24 hours to get to Florida for a funeral. Sorry about that. My grandmother died suddenly after a knee surgery went bad.

Everybody at the Waffle House looks like frazzled drivers, too, and I feel a little better. I order the All Star Special: poached eggs, toast, biscuits & gravy, bacon, and grits for $6.25. The waitress smiles. She asks what I'm writing in my notebook. She's nice. So are the people at the next table, who strike up a conversation. That's the thing about the South: strangers are always saying hello and asking how I'm doing. I don't think they want anything from me, either.

I eat my grits, although I'm not sure what to do with them. Do I add butter? Syrup? Everybody's laughing in deep accents and I can't understand anything they're saying. It's too early. A girl puts a candy bar on my table, smiles, and hurries off. You can smoke here.

Waffle House, Part 2. Six days later, I'm back in North Carolina with a sunburn. Now it's a Waffle House on Truck Stop Road, somewhere near exit 100. I ruminate over my hash brown options. You can get your hash browns scattered, smothered, covered, chunked, peppered, capped, topped, or you can go "all the way." I give up and order the Grilled Texas Bacon Egg & Cheese Melt Plate for $5.85. I sit between a pair of truckers, serious cracked leather men who keep cigarettes burning while eating their biscuits and gravy, reading the paper, and chatting up the waitress.

A big woman shouts about how she wants to smoke and her tiny husband tells her no, it's bad for her and she shouldn't start again. She shoves him hard and says she'll smoke if she goddamn wants. "They say drinking too much water's bad for you, too, so what the hell does anybody know anyway?" Everybody laughs.

The radio says that the senator from Illinois will be arriving in North Carolina tomorrow.

"He's really making the rounds, ain't he?" says the waitress.

"Yep. And I'm glad," says Trucker #1. "Because I still don't know who I'm gonna vote for."

"It's exciting!" says the waitress. "We could have our first black president or our first woman president. I don't know who would do a better job."

Trucker #1 laughs. "Well, it's nice to have options."

Trucker #2 coughs and snaps his paper loudly.

Everybody leaves at the same time. I'm alone in the Waffle House and I don't want to leave, even though my life in New York is waiting ten hours away. But a Waffle House is not a home.

COMMONWEALTH OF PENNSYLVANIA

CITATION NO.

Q 0413362-5

TRAFFIC CITATION / SUMMONS

(570) 356-2309

1. Magisterial District No. 26-3-03

2. Docket Number

3. Address of Magisterial District Office 400 Fisher Ave Catawissa PA 17820

4. Driver Number 45 569 078

5. C.D.L. ☐

6. State ☐ PA ☒ NY

7. D.O.B. 02/02/77

8. Sex ☒ M ☐ F

Last III

9. Defendant Name - First James Middle A Last Reeves III

10. Defendant Address (Street-City-State-Zip Code) 214 Grand St 7 New York NY 10013

11. Veh. Reg. No. CPD435B

12. Reg. Yr. 08

13. State ☐ PA ☒ NY

14. Make Kia

15. Type Sdn

16. Color Silver

17. Veh. Reg. No.

18. Reg. Yr. 08

19. State ☐ PA

20. Make Spectra

21. Type

22. Color

☐ Same as Defendant   ☒ Not Required

23. Owner/Lessee or Carrier Name & Address

VEHICLE CODE
TITLE 75

24. Charge

☒ Maximum Speed Limits
☐ Stop Signs & Yield Signs
☐ Driving Vehicle at Safe Speed
☐ Operation of Vehicle without Official Certificate of Inspection
☐ Driving while Operating Privilege is Suspended or Revoked
☐ Other

☐ Drivers Required to be Licensed
☐ Registration & Certificate of Title Required
☐ Unlawful Activities
☐ Careless Driving
☐ Traffic-Control Signals

26.

27. SEC. 3362 A1.1

28. SUB SEC

29. FINE 76 00

30. E.M.S. 10 00

31. MCARE 40 00

32. COSTS 33 00

33. J.C.P./A.T.J. 10.00

25. Nature of Offense

☒ Speeding 87 MPH   Allowed 65 MPH   ☒ Radar ☐ Clocked ☐ A.O.V.
☐ ESP ☐ Vascar ☐ Other
☐ Operated Vehicle with Expired Inspection
☐ Operated Vehicle with Suspended/Revoked License
☐ Violated 67 Pa. Code
☐ Operated Vehicle without Valid License
☐ Operated Unregistered Vehicle
Ref. 49 CFR

34. TOTAL DUE $ 169 00

☐ Filed on Info. Received

☐ Lab Services Requested

Fines were doubled because: ☐ Highway Safety Corridor ☐ Active Work Zone

35. Location MM 246 WB

36. Zone

39. Code 215

40. Dir. of Travel N S E ☒ W

37. Route RB0

38. Twp.-Boro-City Mifflin Twp

45. Code 19

41. Date 05/01/08

42. Time 1941

43. Day Th

44. County Columbia

47. Date 05/01/08

☒ Issued ☐ Filed

46. Defendant's Signature - Acknowledges Receipt of Citation
X

48. I verify that the facts set forth in this citation are true and correct to the best of my knowledge, information and belief. This verification is made subject to the penalties of Section 4904 of the Crimes Code (18 Pa.C.S. § 4904) relating to unsworn falsification to authorities.

OFFICER'S SIGNATURE Martin

BADGE NO. Zapach 6425/419642

ORI Number PA PSP 0700

49. THIS CITATION HAS BEEN ISSUED/FILED BY A MEMBER OF THE PENNSYLVANIA STATE POLICE, HARRISBURG, PA. 17110.

50. Speed Timing Device Operator Self

51. Miles Followed

52. Miles Timed

53. Secs. Timed

54. Speed Equip. Serial No. FFS937

55. Station Equip. Tested K-8

56. Date Equip. Tested 04/30/08

57. Accident Report No.

58A. Juvenile ☐ YES

58B. Parents Notified ☐ YES ☐ NO

59. Comm. Veh. ☐ YES

60. Haz. Mat. ☐ YES

61. Remarks / Subpoena List 10, LL P Rental Truck Enterprise Rental

62. Special Activity

63. Stop

Obs.

64. Speed Detec. Type

65. Supv. Init.

Badge No.

NOTICE

If you plead guilty or are found guilty, points may be assessed against your driver's record. An accumulation of points may result in the suspension of your driving privilege. Also, your driving privilege WILL BE SUSPENDED if you plead guilty or are found guilty of certain offenses under the Vehicle Code, including but not limited to, 75 Pa.C.S. §§ 1371, 3341, 3345, 3367, 3718, 3733, 3734, 3736, subsequent convictions of 75 Pa.C.S. § 1501, a violation of 75 Pa.C.S. § 3361 when occurring in an active work zone and an accident report is submitted by the police, and a violation of 75 Pa.C.S. § 3362 when occurring in an active work zone.

DEFENDANT   **Q 0413362-5**

SP. 7-0017A
AOPC 406C-95 (Rev. 1/1/2007)

Anatomy of a Speeding Ticket. When I saw the cop, it was too late. He fired up the blue and red lights and pulled into the fast lane. I made a half-assed attempt at hiding, darting between two trucks and slowing down to sixty, but the fuzz was already next to my window, making sharp gestures to pull over.

There was no small talk with this guy, no "Do you know why I stopped you?" or "What seems to be the hurry?" He only said, "License and registration, please." I handed over my paperwork and told him that I don't normally speed, that I was just trying to get around that U-Haul back there.

"You were going 87 miles per hour."

"Wow. Can you let me go with a warning?"

He didn't look at me, just put his sunglasses back on and returned to his car with my paperwork. Why does it take so long for them to write a ticket? What are they doing back there? I always worry that the cop computer pulls up a list of every dumb thing I've ever done, things I thought nobody else saw, and he's sitting back there laughing his ass off. But maybe they just want to destroy your ETA.

Ten minutes later, he comes back with my ticket and tells me that I have fourteen days to pay it or else there will be a warrant and other problems. "Be careful getting back on the highway." I fight back the impulse to say "thank you." I always say "thank you" after I get a ticket and spend the rest of my trip regretting it.

My ticket was $169.50, which seemed more expensive than usual. Apparently, Pennsylvania has tacked on a bunch of pork to feed its state machinery, which is identified only by a series of cryptic acronyms. Curious about where my money was going, I looked them up.

$76.00 - Basic fine for going 22 miles over the posted limit.

$10.00 - **EMT** - The Emergency Medical Services Act, which was passed in October 2006 to underwrite ambulances because Pennsylvania decided it was "in the public interest to assure that there are high quality and coordinated emergency and urgent medical services readily available to prevent premature death and reduce suffering and disability that arise from severe illness and injury..."

$40.00 - **MCARE** - Medical Care Availability and Reduction of Error Fund. Passed in 2002, this fee goes toward "reducing the cost of medical professional liability insurance to ensure that medical care is available in this Commonwealth through a comprehensive and high-quality health care system."

$33.00 - "Costs." No idea.

$10.00 - **J.C.P./A.T.J.** - Judicial Computer Project / Access to Justice. This righteous -sounding penalty buys better computers for Pennsylvania's court clerks. The press release offers a vague notion of how improved technology will enhance "the ability to quickly access the most current court information throughout the state — information including prior convictions, bail history, pending charges and outstanding warrants..."

To the good people of Pennsylvania, you are very welcome. Enjoy your low insurance rates and fancy computers.

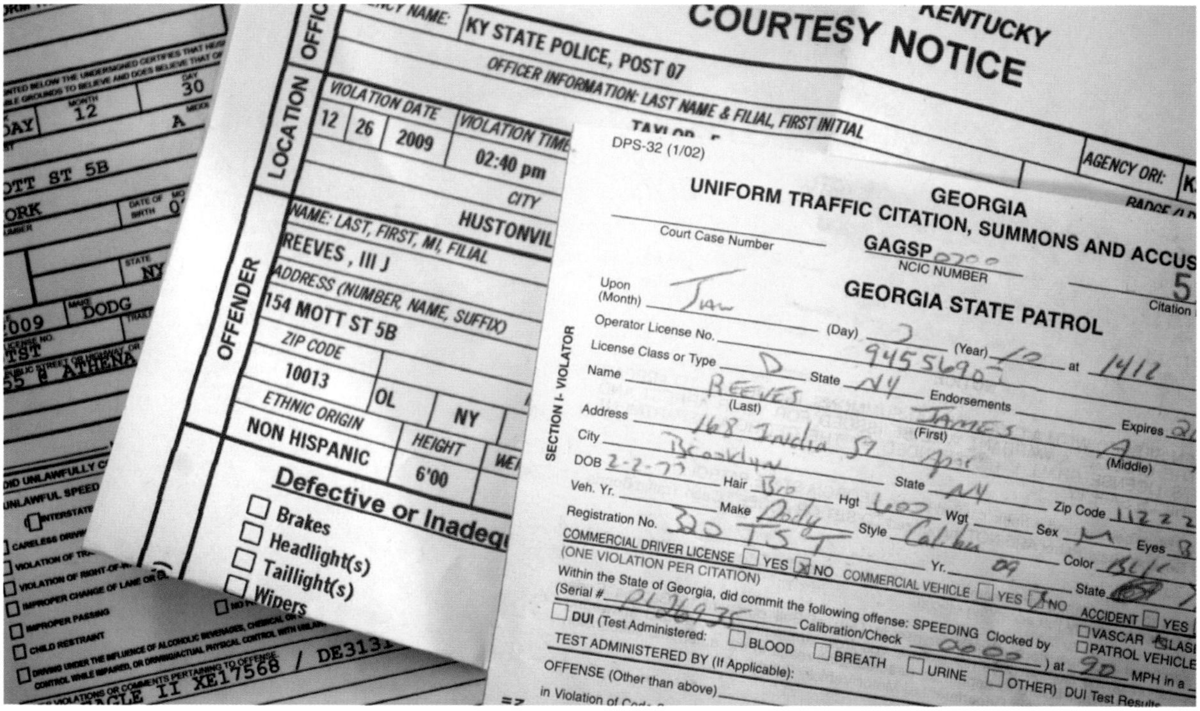
KENTUCKY
COURTESY NOTICE
KY STATE POLICE, POST 07
OFFICER INFORMATION: LAST NAME & FILIAL, FIRST INITIAL
LOCATION
VIOLATION DATE
12 26 2009
VIOLATION TIME
02:40 pm
CITY
HUSTONVIL
OFFENDER
NAME: LAST, FIRST, MI, FILIAL
REEVES , III J
ADDRESS (NUMBER, NAME, SUFFIX)
154 MOTT ST 5B
ZIP CODE
10013
OL
NY
ETHNIC ORIGIN
NON HISPANIC
HEIGHT
6'00
Defective or Inadequ
Brakes
Headlight(s)
Taillight(s)
Wipers
AGENCY ORI:
DPS-32 (1/02)
GEORGIA
UNIFORM TRAFFIC CITATION, SUMMONS AND ACCUS
Court Case Number
GAGSP
NCIC NUMBER
GEORGIA STATE PATROL
SECTION I- VIOLATOR
Upon (Month)
Operator License No.
(Day)
(Year)
at
License Class or Type
State
Name
Endorsements
(Last)
(First)
(Middle)
Address
Expires
City
DOB
Hair
State
Veh. Yr.
Make
Hgt
Wgt
Zip Code
Registration No.
Style
Sex
Eyes
COMMERCIAL DRIVER LICENSE
YES
NO
COMMERCIAL VEHICLE
(ONE VIOLATION PER CITATION)
Yr.
Color
Within the State of Georgia, did commit the following offense: SPEEDING
Clocked by
State
(Serial #
Calibration/Check
ACCIDENT
DUI (Test Administered:
BLOOD
BREATH
URINE
OTHER)
VASCAR
PATROL VEHICLE
TEST ADMINISTERED BY (If Applicable):
MPH in a
OFFENSE (Other than above)
DUI Test Results
MOTT ST 5B
DODG
ATHENA
XE17568 / DE313

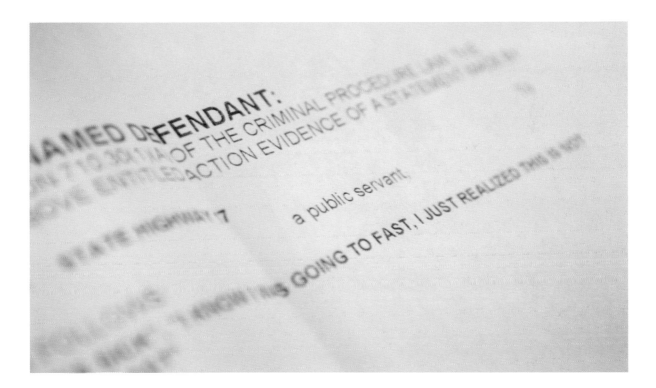

American Moment. Somewhere along the border of Nevada and Utah, a fat man wearing hospital pants and no shirt grills some steaks on the back of his dented Airstream Classic trailer. Old missile casings and rusted fuselages sit in his backyard, which is an endless desert thundering out toward the Sierra Nevada range.

I pull over and take my zillionth picture of the sinking sun. The man calls out *howdy* and I shout *hey*, our voices bouncing off the hills. The air is dead silent except for the sizzle of the Coleman grill fifty yards into the weeds. A screen door bangs and he disappears and returns with more steaks.

I often dream about pointing the car at California and driving into the setting sun. Do people who live out west ever fantasize about driving to New York or Boston? I scan the horizon, thinking I can almost see Detroit and all the way down to New Orleans and across to Los Angeles. This country is too damned big. A small panic rushes up. Who installed these power lines way the hell out here? Or are they telephone cables? I don't understand how anything works.

Four hundred and six miles to go. My rental car sprays dust and the fat man waves as I push south toward Vegas.

Scenery. I'm too self-conscious to enjoy the Grand Canyon correctly. Or Yosemite or Joshua Tree or Big Sur or Yellowstone. Standing at the edge of this impossible scenery, I realize that I've looked at this picture too many times even though I have never been here. This is the stuff of calendar photographs and inspirational posters and, now that I'm standing in front of it, I'm trying too hard to make it matter. I expect to be overwhelmed by the beauty of nature, to feel the stirring of a new spiritual connection or to forge some kind of peace before ambling back to my car as a newly minted man, happy and humbled after glimpsing his place in this wild universe.

I wait for this moment but it never comes. And if it does, the soundtrack isn't right: there's the sound of crunching gravel or a girl snapping her gum or noisy families angling for a group photo rather than the melancholy strings or lonely wind that the scenery deserves. Still, it's a pretty spot when the sun sets: everything gets very orange and pink.

Flags. Patriotism is strange. There was a time not too long ago when it was considered bad form to fly the flag at night. When I was small, my grandfather taught me how to fold the flag into a tight little triangle. He told me that I should take down the flag when it rains and I should never let it touch the ground.

Now it's plastered on every truck and car. It flies across advertisements for casinos, hardware stores, car dealerships, stadiums, and adult video outlets. It's painted on the sides of barns, spray-painted on the flanks of cows, draped across mountaintops, and pinned to the lapels of our politicians. If any other country were going this flag crazy, I imagine we would get a bit jumpy.

There are war machines out there in America. Along the far edges of county roads and rural routes, old towns are built out of monuments to war. In Kansas you'll find a bronzed tank sitting on a lawn, pointed at a shuttered main street while dark factories loom silently in the background. In Alabama you'll see towering slabs of polished granite and marble list the names of men who died fighting Mexico, Germany, Japan, Korea, Vietnam, and Iraq. These memorials are out of scale with the beaten trailers and peeling ranch houses that surround them. Flags, ribbons, and stickers are stuck to every other truck and car. *These colors don't run. Don't tread on me. Love it or leave it. Mess with the best, die like the rest. Happiness is a belt-fed weapon.* Burning towers are painted across a dead train trestle in Wyoming with red and blue bubble letters that say *We will never forget. Hoo ah.*

It's good to love your community, but loving your nation can be scary.

Blanket of Freedom. In the lobby of a Walmart in Pahrump, Nevada, there are dozens of framed portraits of young local men and women in military dress. Above the sliding doors, big silver letters say *My son is standing watch tonight so that you and I may sleep under a blanket of Freedom.*

When did freedom become capitalized? Strange, this business of war. It's in our supermarkets, stuck to our bumpers, and pinned to our lapels, yet I still have trouble accepting that I live in a warlike country. But war is in our DNA: our national anthem is packed with heavy artillery. We repress any memories of the people who lived here first and we spin romantic story lines out of a messy civil war. World War I was confusing. World War II was the good war. Nobody remembers the Korean War. Vietnam was a bad war. After that, war became remote, moving from the efforts of citizens into the hands of paid professionals.

In 1942, my grandfather landed in France where he operated radar equipment. Tell people that your grandfather served in World War II and you're met with a quiet nod. A hushed weight. Toughness and goodness drew a halo around America during the 1940s and we cling to it seventy years later. Driving through Ohio, I flip on the radio and hear a man yelling: "Arrogance? Was America *arrogant* when we liberated France and rescued the world from a tyrant?" This is the lunatic chatter of a bloated fighter reliving his glory days, forever trying to fight the same championship bout even though the match is over and the rules changed long ago.

And yet I recently stood in Grenoble looking at statues of Roosevelt and Churchill with a French and a German friend — and the war felt very close as we talked about grandparents. This was during the days of Freedom Fries, those strange days when the House of Representatives ordered its cafeteria to serve Freedom Toast. I try to imagine what my grandfather, an eighteen-year-old kid at the time, thought about France as he left behind college, a fiancée, and a job to pick up a gun and land on an icy shore in the middle of the night. When I was eighteen, I was smoking a lot of weed and switching my major from Japanese Literature to Film & Video Studies.

For years I quizzed my grandfather about the war, pressing for the gory details: Did you kill anybody? Were you scared? He would give a short laugh and say something like, "Jimmy, now that you mention it, I remember this one lieutenant of ours. Hell of a guy. Why, he could . . ." and off he would go, telling me stories about the uncanny math skills of his lieutenant, about the abominable hygiene of his bunkmate, and the mysterious radar equipment. He told me about drinking dusty wine in abandoned châteaus with famous paintings still hanging from the walls. "Sometimes we lived like lords," he said. He told me about everything except for the war itself and it would take years before I caught on. He was never going to discuss what happened there. And so the image of my grandfather in France is a static one: carrying candles from room to room in a flickering old castle, trying to make out the details of a family portrait while hell came down outside. He was eighteen years old.

War machines. I'm staring at war machines in the hard Alabama sun. A few miles outside of Mobile, there's a well-groomed park filled with retired tanks, bombers, battleships, and heavy artillery. This is a place for Americans to eat lunch and relax among their weapons. The USS Alabama looms large in Mobile Bay while families picnic next to anti-aircraft cannons and fighter jets. I wave at a cheerful man on a ladder who's touching up the paint job on a Blackbird spy plane. Gun turrets point at Interstate 10 and a Sherman tank sits next to a swing set.

Race. I want to believe that things are different these days and maybe they are. I grew up a few miles outside of Detroit, a city where the racial lines are drawn so bold and deep that nobody can overlook them. And after teaching in New York City's public schools, I couldn't help but think about race all the time. But my first trip down South brought it home hard. Somber historical markers and bronze statues can't erase the past. Not when an old black man tapped me on the shoulder in Birmingham. "See that fountain?" he asked. "When I was a boy, I couldn't drink from it. That was the white man's fountain."

All I could say to the man was *God, this actually happened here, we actually lived this way,* and the man grabbed my shoulder hard and swung me around. "Of course it happened! See that church? That's where they blew up those little girls."

Towne Village Centre. Sometimes there are towns with no name, only a metroplex of today's biggest brands: Target, Mervyn's, Staples, a Starbucks, Walmart Super Center, Kohl's, Applebee's, Jo-Anne's Fabrics, and so on. Some stores are in strip malls, others are freestanding boxes, and all of it is surrounded by a mad ocean of parking spaces dotted with medians, loops, and traffic-calming shrubs.

You ping-pong around this thing, making fugitive cuts across the painted lines, trying to determine the best sequence for buying batteries, socks, a cup of coffee, and swearing you saw a Radio Shack somewhere although you might just be assuming it's here. Everything blurs together in a calculated blend of beige and gray anonymity. Bed Bath & Beyond, Red Lobster, Office Max, Chili's. Take a wrong turn behind the glued-on shingles and fake old-timey shutters, and you realize the other three sides of these buildings are a dead-eyed concrete afterthought that is not designed for public viewing: loading docks, tangles of utility cables, dumpsters, and employee parking.

These shopping centers are everywhere and nobody likes them. Nobody will fall in love here. Dignity and pride are not in the design. Words like "plaza" and "village commons" and "towne centre" are often attached to the signs, but they read like a dark joke. Sometimes there are benches but nobody sits on them unless they're waiting for someone to pull the car around. Why not stack all of these stores on top of one another and put them in a row? You'd have a decent little Main Street town.

Megamarket. You can buy a shotgun, a gerbil, a bottle of scotch, some yogurt, Band-Aids, and tennis shoes in one trip. My cart glides across buffed linoleum while I search and consider and judge and reject. I troll the fluorescent aisles at midnight with the stoned and sleepless as I search for a blender and electric toothbrush. Last week I bought an iron, business socks, and a pumpkin pie.

There is no subtlety in the detergent aisle: All. Era. Gain. Cheer. Bold. Existential, supersaturated. I'm dazzled by the yards of eggs, snapping photographs of thirty kinds of milk, looking for a pair of driving gloves. I spend fifteen minutes staring at shampoo. Ultra-moisturizing. Cool menthol aroma. Ice shine. Natural fusion. Clear & clarifying. Herbal-based. Oil-based. Water-based. Shampoo for combination hair. An associate asks me if I need help and I do, but I'm too overwhelmed to answer. Scalp control. Smooth vitality. Breakage defense. Panic sets in. There is too much of everything beneath five city blocks of unforgiving glare. I go home in a daze but later that night I return. I buy a jigsaw puzzle and some lime juice at three in the morning.

Parade. A ribbon of sequins, latex, bare skin, and heavy makeup snakes down Surf Avenue. Thousands of New Yorkers climb over one another to get a better look. Inspired by Coney Island's Mardi Gras celebration during its heydey back in the 1920s, the Mermaid Parade first marched down the boardwalk in 1983 and it's been NYC's unofficial summer kickoff ever since.

There are mermaids, zombies, jellyfish, robots, cowgirls, and topless women in tassles and wigs. You'll see French maids, lizards, kids in swim fins, swamp monsters, and old people dressed up as woodland creatures. They pose and grin for the sweaty crowd while the judges demand more beer over the PA system and people scream from the Cyclone and Tilt-a-Whirl overhead.

Weird energy fills the salty air because everybody knows that these might be the last days of Coney Island. Developers are descending with plans to sterilize and modernize — they want to transform the home of a game called *Shoot the Freak (Live Human Target!)* into a climate-controlled Las Vegas, and the neighborhood is fighting hard to keep its deep fried soul. But today the freak flags fly and everyone looks beautiful and I wonder why we don't dress up like this every day.

Parade, Part II. One night I sat in the backseat of a car heading to a Honduran restaurant somewhere deep in New Orleans. Turning onto St. Bernard Avenue in the Seventh Ward, we ran smack into a thumping racket: feathers flew, beads sparkled, headlights flashed, and people beat on drums. The driver screamed "Look, it's the Indians!" and hit the brakes and jumped out of the car.

We followed the crowd. Costumed men thundered in towering plumes and capes, stomping and swooshing and chanting. Incense and dope smoke clouded the streetlights and people hollered as we snaked through neighborhoods that have been historically beaten up and flooded. These are the Mardi Gras Indians, and every year they march in jaw-dropping costumes around midnight on the eve of St. Joseph's Day.

They've been doing it since the 1870s and the origins of the tradition are mysterious: some say it originated from an affinity between Africans and Native Americans, as well as an attempt by black people to skirt segregation laws by disguising themselves as Indians. Another story says that the tradition began as a tribute to American Indians who helped runaway slaves, and Buffalo Bill's Wild West show in the 1880s was said to have sparked interest in dressing up as Indians for Mardi Gras. The handcrafted costumes are elaborately embroidered, bejeweled, and constructed with a level of care that you don't often see these days, and for a few nights they go out into the world before being sold to collectors for thousands of dollars. And they're worth it, simply for drawing the city together and creating such wild energy on St. Bernard Avenue in the middle of the night.

Invasion. Nationalism is on my mind in Idaho. I saw a billboard along the interstate advertising Dan Adamson for governor: a sturdy man in a wide suit, flashing a sparkling grin and standing next to fat red letters declaring that "Idaho is for Idahoans." Sounds good, but what does that mean? Perhaps this has something to do with the banners reading "Keep Illegal Immigrants Out" and "American Jobs for Americans" that are draped across small towns in Kansas, Colorado, and Utah.

A strange isolationism has been creeping around the nation since September 11, and Idaho is kicking it up a notch. *Idaho is for Idahoans.* No argument there. Sounds tough but expresses nothing except paranoia. It'd be far more interesting if Dan announced that "Montana is for Idahoans." Now there's something to get excited about. Why don't states invade each other anymore?

Things You Can Kill on the Road (and Vice Versa). There's a lot to worry about when driving America's back roads, particularly west of the continental divide. Yellow signs warn about dust hazards, rough roads, uneven shoulders, steep grades, sudden storms, high winds, fresh oil, falling rocks, all accompanied by nerve-racking illustrations of your car tipping over or plunging into a canyon. But it's the animals that really make me nervous.

On the east coast, sometimes you'll see a sign for deer and it's usually taken as a remote possibility, as in *somebody spotted a deer here a few years ago, so we put up this sign*. In states like Colorado and Wyoming, however, these signs mean *at least a dozen of these things will jump in front of your car tonight*. Maybe a deer, or some cattle, elk, wild dogs, scorpions, snakes, and a few animals that I can't identify. Cougars? Bison? Sometimes the Department of Transportation throws up its hands and simply installs a sign that says: "General Wildlife Crossing, Next 31 Miles."

Here's a brief inventory of the things that I've killed over the course of 50,000 miles: two birds, eight rabbits, two skunks, one raccoon, one scorpion (in the car after it stung me on the neck), several mice, possibly a porcupine, and countless bugs filled with neon juice. Things that have almost killed me: five deer, three cows, two bison, and countless rabbits (and eventually I gave up trying to avoid them).

State Line. Note the buckshot in this sign. A good rule of thumb is that the more bullet holes a state sign has, the scarier the state. The worst I've seen are Texas, Arkansas, and Nevada. North Dakota falls somewhere in the middle. Nevada was swiss cheese.

There ought to be more of a to-do when crossing state lines. You'd think each state would seize this opportunity to put on a bit of a show with colorful signs and exciting slogans, maybe even a few people who wave and throw confetti and float giant balloons. At the very least, they might not want to advertise that their citizens are heavily armed.

Tower. You can speed through a lot of America and see nothing but grids of green and brown, nothing but corn and pump jacks and corn and rusted trains and more corn. And just when you're thinking that you understand the term *flyover country*, you drive into a town like Bartlesville and wonder what else you've been speeding past. A former oil boom town in the northeast corner of Oklahoma, Bartlesville is the birthplace of Phillips Petroleum. It's also where Frank Lloyd Wright's only skyscraper stands.

Wright's tower was originally designed as a Manhattan apartment building for St. Mark's Place until the Great Depression and clashing personalities killed the project. Twenty-five years later, Harold C. Price contacted Wright about building the headquarters for his burgeoning pipeline operation in Bartlesville. Wright dusted off the blueprints and went to work, apparently unaware that he was building in Oklahoma rather than the Bowery. Christened the Price Tower, Wright dubbed it "the tree that escaped the forest." Not only does the tower stand in the middle of open prairie rather than among the clutter of lower Manhattan, it's built upon a modular structure of cantilevered concrete "branches," forming a cramped interior that would make perfect sense in New York but feels claustrophobic on the Great Plains.

Notorious for appearing on his former clients' doorsteps to rearrange the furniture and toss their trinkets, Wright was no different with Price. If the CEO must keep a globe in his office, Wright demanded that it be hidden behind the door so as not to interfere with his beloved triangles. Triangles are everywhere in the Price Tower: three rooms to a floor, each devoid of any right angles. And because this is a Wright building, every minor detail bears his touch: the shower is a triangle stall, the wastebasket is a triangle that slots neatly into the 60-degree angle formed by the legs of the desk, the copper facade is echoed in the copper furniture, the copper mesh curtains, and the copper lighting fixtures. And now you can sleep here, following a renovation into a hotel and arts center.

The Price Tower is a fascinating building, but it's Bartlesville that sticks in my mind: it's a short walk to the Phillips Petroleum Museum, a handful of cheap diners, and a classic Main Street awkwardly caught in postindustrial transition. To complement the tower, Bartlesville is courting top-shelf architects for additional buildings, aggressively buying up blueprints and journals for its architecture library, and there is optimistic chatter about transforming Bartlesville into a playground for architects and artists. The housing crisis put the freeze on many of these plans but, whether or not they come to pass, it's comforting to know you can drive like mad across the plains, stumble into a Frank Lloyd Wright building in the middle of the night, and wake up the next morning to listen to an elderly lady in a Kansas City Chiefs jersey rhapsodize about Zaha Hadid's Rosenthal Center for Contemporary Art before you tour a corporate museum dedicated to the bootstrapping spirit of an oil company. Something about Bartlesville tells me that America's going to be all right.

Banging on Cars in the Dakotas. Sometimes I feel jumpy, spooked by the few people that I pass when driving through shuttered small towns. The kids look wild, glaring at me and shouting at a red light. Skinny hard-bodied guys without shirts and chubby girls with cleavage spilling everywhere. They burn rubber, bang the sides of their cars, and hang out in gas station parking lots, sitting in pickup beds, whooping and throwing cans.

A few factories spit fire into the night, but most of them are rusted-up monsters, gigantic cylinders and cones and boxes beyond the tracks that make a ghostly skyline behind an empty Main Street. Some of the towns vibrate like something awful happened. The only place to eat is a Pizza Hut. Five years ago, my waiter worked on his family's farm with his dad. Now the farm is gone and he's waiting tables and he's pissed. He talks about the empty buildings and predatory agribusiness. It's the first time I ever heard somebody mention meth.

I take photographs of scrap yards and busted homes. I get skittish. I feel criminal, stealing images of beat-up towns and dead industry and driving away.

Dinosaur. After a harrowing night drive through the Rocky Mountains, I wasn't sure where to go next. I pulled over, flipped on the interior light, and scanned my atlas. I noticed a town called Dinosaur on the map. Although it was in the opposite corner of the state, I became fixated on waking up in Dinosaur the next morning. Where else was I going to go? So I drove like mad through the night on a frightening mountain road that quickly disappeared from the map, giving way to open ranges with cows sleeping in the road, falling rocks, signs riddled with bullet holes, and curves that made ten miles per hour seem reckless. At three in the morning, the car was crunching over rabbits.

"Yeah, these roads are crawling with rabbits 'round springtime," said the old man who ran the only motel in Dinosaur. He wore a bathrobe and smelled like sleep. "What the hell are you doing out here anyway?"

"This town is called Dinosaur. Who wouldn't come?"

"Nobody comes here," he said, handing me the key. "But enjoy yourself just the same." He shuffled off to bed.

I woke up in a world of scorched rock, burnt scrub grass, and 106° sun. Originally known as Artesia, the town changed its name to Dinosaur in 1966 to capitalize on its proximity to the Dinosaur National Monument, a 200,000-acre quarry that spans the Utah and Colorado border. With a population of 319, it's a tough little collection of trailers on streets called Brontosaurus Boulevard, Triceratops Terrace, and Diplodocus Drive. A few dinosaur statues sat in the middle of town, relics of an abandoned tourist attraction from back when families took road trips. The only place to eat was an old diner with the curtains drawn and a faded *For Sale* sign in the window. Empty, save for an old man who stared as the door jingled open.

"Can I sit anywhere?"

He nodded. He had a handlebar mustache and wore a John Deere cap. "Our deep fryer's broken," he said. "No fries, fish, or chicken."

"That's good news for my arteries."

No response.

"I'll just have a ham and cheese sandwich."

He returned with my sandwich. "Sorry about the fryer. The gas line's busted and I haven't been able to get anybody to come out here to take a look at it."

I asked him about dinosaurs.

"Yeah, there's a canyon where they dug up all them fossils. Go look at it. Or don't." He had other things on his mind.

As I headed out of town, a fat man in a baseball cap, tucked-in polo shirt, and a red gym bag stood at the side of the road waving his thumb. As I sped past him, he slapped his jeans with a sad little smack and hollered "Fuck." I watched him rage in the rearview and felt a little guilty for leaving a man behind.

Chasing Cosmic Rays in a Rental Car. Delta is one of the last towns in Utah before the big blank sheets of the Great Basin get under way. I speed past crumbling buildings that were once pharmacies and hardware stores. A vinyl sign hangs from an old gas station with blue siding. It says "Lon and Mary Watson Millard County Cosmic Ray Center." I hit the brakes.

The whitewashed garage is littered with rusted debris from a former life as an auto repair shop. A few charts are pinned to a bulletin board and four Asian kids sit at card tables, hunched over laptops and graph paper. Keyboard chatter stops cold. All eyes are on me. I wave hello. "I'm sure you're asked this a lot, but what are cosmic rays?"

"Nobody asks that," says a girl near the back. "Nobody comes here."

I stare at the kids and they stare at me. We're puzzled by each other's presence in the Cosmic Ray Center. I expected to find a hippie spirituality outfit, perhaps something involving crystals and meditation, and God knows what I looked like to them, stumbling through their door after speeding across the desert floor for seven hours with the windows down.

They huddle. After a flurry of Japanese whispers, a spindly guy in a Chicago Bulls t-shirt is elected to deal with me. He says they're searching for cosmic rays from the sun and the Great Basin is one of the only places flat and wide enough to find them.

"Japan is too small," he says. "So we come here."

"And how do you like Utah?"

He smiles politely and shrugs, then points at the charts, chattering about vectors and particles and detectors. I begin to drift, although I make a show of jotting down some notes because I think that he thinks I might be official. Later I sit in the car frowning at my notebook: *Sun. Universe. Mirrors. Energy beams. Chicago Bulls. Complex hand gestures . . .*

The Cosmic Ray Center is the staging area for the Telescope Array Experiment, which, according to a trifold brochure, "is designed to observe cosmic-ray-induced air showers at extremely high energies using a combination of ground array and air-fluorescence techniques. The cosmic rays are observed at three fluorescence sites and a separate ground array consisting of 576 detectors. Understanding the origin of the highest-energy cosmic rays is one of the great unanswered questions in fundamental physics."

The Telescope Array is a shared effort between several research facilities in America, Japan, Korea, and Russia. The collaboration with the University of Tokyo is striking because the site of the Topaz War Relocation Center sits only a few miles away. More than 10,000 Japanese-Americans were imprisoned here during World War II. There was barbed wire and there were vegetable gardens. They had a high school, a baseball team, a literary journal, and armed sentries on the roof. It was first known as the Central Utah Relocation Center, but this name was quickly ditched when people began referring to the place by its acronym: "Curse." The camp was temporarily rechristened "Delta" until the town's Mormon residents refused to be associated with a prison. It was finally named after a nearby mountain, which did not complain.

The kid in the jersey talks about air showers and radiation. I flash on the hangar that housed the *Enola Gay*, the B-29 that dropped Little Boy on Japan. In the northwest corner of the state, I wandered into an abandoned army barracks where the people from the Center for Land Use Interpretation took me for a walk. Shrapnel and bomb fins were buried in the dirt, and the hangar was an unsettling sight because it was nothing more than a rusted aluminum shed rotting in the sun, an anonymous structure that produced a machine that left 200,000 people dead on the other side of the world.

A dramatic *Citizen Kane* shot: I gaze past the kid and squint at the celestial light beating at a window that frames a deep focus square of endless blond rock and shocking blue sky. The desert overwhelms me. What goes on in all of this space? If I keep driving along Route 50, I'll reach the margins of Area 51 where there's a gas station that sells alien jerky to tourists. Keep driving and there's a makeshift bar with grainy photographs of mysterious lights tacked to the walls and chicken wire strapped across the bottles to protect the booze from sonic booms. All of this hot empty space teems with prisons, bombs, aliens, razor wire, and clandestine operations. Last night on the radio somebody said the president and his family might be clones of a race of ancient pharaohs who are preparing for an interstellar war. Somebody else called to say that the lost city of Atlantis was at 39.52° N, which is exactly the same latitude as Reno. The radio host whistled knowingly. It was all connected.

In the quiet garage, I squint at the charts tracking the habits of cosmic rays. The lanky kid tells me that his detectors cover more than five hundred miles and the beams are recorded using mirrors. Right now there are five hundred machines in the desert scanning the sky for beams from outer space. "One day we hope that cosmic rays can be harnessed as an energy source," he says. People looking for good vibes. I like that. Maybe things are going in the right direction. I run out of questions and wish him luck. Everybody waves enthusiastically as I drive into the middle of nowhere, wondering what else people are doing out here.

The Delta. A heavy purple heat sits on you in Mississippi. Driving along the river on Route 1, there's a wild moon so big and red that for a moment I think I'm looking at the sunset. Heat lightning. The sky flashes and strobes like evil, which seems right: this is strange land, this is the Deep South, a phrase that vibrates with rumor and legend and scorn. They say this is where Robert Johnson sold his soul to the devil for guitar skills. They say a lot of things about the Delta. It's dark and the insects scream and sometimes I see fires burning in oil drums in front of trailer bars.

Just outside of Greenville, red and blue lights dazzle and the police have four men on their knees, hands to their heads. Then it's deep brush and dark swamp again. My headlights pass over a car door, beaten shacks, a dead turkey. A school bus sawed in half lengthwise charges down the dusty road. I hear screams and laughter, and it rumbles into the dark. Three in the morning and I'm the only soul. The heat lightning gets frantic and I pull over next to the river, kill the lights, and stand in the road, watching the sky flash.

I wake up in Natchez, which is beautiful and desolate on Sunday. Maybe this old redbrick and tin town was left for dead. Maybe everybody's in church or sleeping something off. My footsteps echo down the boiling asphalt. A small soul food restaurant is the only thing open. The man behind the counter has some fun because I don't know what a neckbone is. I order catfish and mustard greens. Gospel plays softly from the kitchen and a little boy wipes down the tables, singing to himself. He drops into the booth across from me and quizzes me about my camera. He says he wants to be a photographer and travel the world taking pictures of snakes. Rattlesnakes. King cobras. Black mambas. Water moccasins. He knows a lot about snakes and how to photograph them.

"But that'll never happen." He looks around the restaurant and leans across the table and whispers, "Because I'll probably get killed."

I think of those flashing police lights in the swampy night, the people glaring drunkenly from paint-peeled porches, the title pawn and gun shops on the edge of town.

"Why?" I ask

"I have bad luck," he says. "I'll probably get bitten by a snake."

Landing at Louis Armstrong for a fast weekend visit. The highway to New Orleans features billboards promising naked women on stage, on video, on a pole, most of which are for "little darlings" or "barely legal co-eds." Sometimes it's mortifying to be a man. The sprawl ends sharp once you see the Superdome. My eyes greedily scan for damage, but downtown New Orleans is as beautiful as when I left it last August, two weeks before everything fell apart. It's a fascinating and honest city, like few others in America.

Stepping into the wet electric heat, you never forget that New Orleans was built on a swamp. The only benefit is the affectation of patting one's brow with a folded handkerchief. In the French Quarter, I have to go to three stores before I find a lighter that is not shaped like a penis or has flashing LED nipples. The elderly architecture is stunning: red, blue, orange wood, and old black Spanish ironwork with green ferns dripping everywhere. On Bourbon Street there is the sour mud smell of fresh vomit. Girls go wild on the balcony, pulling at their tight shirts while waving enormous drinks in fluorescent plastic cups. If it weren't for the *Fuck FEMA* t-shirts and handwritten signs announcing that such-and-such has been cleared by the health authorities to reopen, I would never guess that something bad happened here. Then I walk outside the Quarter.

Walking east in the brutal afternoon, I plotted a checkered course determined by rare patches of shade, stopping every few blocks for a bottle of water and a cigarette. A thin and nervous man on a bicycle told me that he was a high school music teacher and now he's homeless and riding the streets, waiting until the government tells him he can return to his house or an ID card arrives that will allow him to stay at one of the few functioning shelters in the city. Whichever comes first. After telling his story and declining a cigarette, he rode off. "Have a nice vacation in New Orleans!" he yelled.

Although I walked for hours, I made it only to the edge of the Ninth Ward. A tangle of highway, bridge, and canal kept me walking in circles around several empty blocks, and I was not used to the heat. Delirium forced a retreat back to the west, where people worked on their houses, cleaning and hammering, and soon back to the stores and bars and antiques shops where it looked like everything might be okay for the city after all.

I did not see anything close to the worst of it, but I saw enough to shake my faith in the idea that things will be okay, that there are people in charge. Seeing a wrecked building feels like a body blow. A sucker punch. There's a physical response, like looking at a horrible deformity or an open wound. I drove around New Orleans on a Monday morning, shocked to see all of the untouched damage from two years ago: the collapsed frameworks, the towers of garbage, the handwritten shouts and prayers spray-painted across the brick and wood: *Please Pick Up the Trash. U Loot, U Dead. 2 Cats Found. FEMA Go to Hell.*

Trees on top of houses, cars on top of trees. Shards of wood and aluminum, broken glass, thickets of wires, mountains of garbage, and cryptic markings spray-painted next to the front door of every house: a cross with dates, numbers, mysterious acronyms (TWF means "toxic waste found," e.g., bodies inside), and the heartbreaking *two cats* or *dog found* . . . these symbols hit the hardest, conjuring black-and-white images of long-ago wars and distant genocides. Nobody writes on doors when things are going well.

In New York City, "exclusive living" condo towers, elaborately themed bars, and exotic tennis shoe galleries arrive in regular waves. Last month I drove through the suburbs of Virginia, stunned by the brand-new shopping centers, disposable strip malls, and vacant office parks. These new buildings just show up in the middle of the night.

Katrina hit a long time ago.

Venice Jump Basin. What's on those little fingers of land that spread out below New Orleans? The map lists towns with names such as Port Sulphur, Triumph, and Happy Jack. I head south on Highway 11 in search of quirky bayou scenery and colorful stories, but the scene is ripped to shreds: a looping strip of bashed tin roofs, gnarled sheds, and skeletal buildings. Stern government signs urge residents to complete their home inspections before federal cleanup begins.

I push south and the line between poverty and hurricane damage becomes difficult to decipher, blurring for nearly fifty miles: a string of fishing towns beaten by storms and everything else God and man could throw at them. Wrecked houses stand on stilts, stubbornly challenging the next storm. And when you get to the very bottom of Louisiana, there's a thrilling and repulsive skyline of metal glittering like something peeled off a Fritz Lang backdrop. Jimi Hendrix does "Voodoo Chile" on the radio while helicopters chop overhead, yellow booms swing across docks, and big fire shoots into the sky.

Welcome to the Venice Jump Basin, a sun-soaked and mosquito-infested network of oil refineries, boom cranes, freighters, frigates, and cargo docks. These are the guts of American energy. Halliburton, Texaco, Chevron, British Petroleum, and US Liquid Plastics are all here, dredging and pumping and refining and shipping. And none of these corporations could kick a few dollars up the road to put a new roof on the grocery store?

Gulf. Driving along the coast on a Monday night, I zoom through a schizophrenic strip of shocking poverty and sparkling development. There's gorgeous sand in Mississippi, broad empty beaches just west of Gulfport. Mansions float on stilts above crumpled sheds and bridges wrecked from the storms two years ago. Biloxi is a tangle of highway and parkway, all of it leading to new casinos. The sun sets as I stand among a battered cluster of Vietnamese markets, temples, and shops with signs cursing the government.

On Tuesday morning I'm in Mobile, where all of the beautiful buildings stand empty. The features of a city are here, but there's no bustle. Where did everybody go? A woman in a pantsuit pushes a shopping cart through the park, handing out brown bag lunches to dazed people propped on benches. They ignore her, waiting until she leaves before peeking inside the bags.

I drive past bulldozer rental stations and Northrop Grumman Shop Systems. I marvel at the hulking Chevron and Texaco refineries. A cemetery lives next door to a junkyard. So many junkyards. The bodies of our cars keep piling up along the fringes. After driving for ten days, I could publish photographs of busted machines and dead buildings for decades.

Little old ladies drive enormous pickup trucks. A gay pride sticker sits next to the Confederate flag on somebody's bumper. I live in a beautiful nation of car dealerships and panic attacks. I pull over and eat a Whataburger at a rest stop just east of Pensacola.

Point Taken. I pull up to a dusty cinder-block box in the middle of the desert that says "Bar" and open the steel door on a dark and empty room with a bar at the back. Everything's in disarray, like they're just moving in or moving out, although the proprietor looks like he's been here for centuries.

"You open?" I ask.

"Sit down," he says.

I order a ginger ale and he grunts and slams a can of Canada Dry on the bar. "Where you from?"

"New York."

"So what on earth are you doing here?"

"Road trip. Seeing America."

"Now why the hell would you come all the way out here when you've got all of America right there at home?"

AM Radio Scan. "Over three hundred bodies were taken to the mosque on Saturday. It's unclear how many Christians were killed since their remains were not taken to a mosque. An around-the-clock curfew has been imposed on the city, which has a long history of violence. Fighting followed the first local election in more than a decade, beginning as clashes between the political parties when electoral workers failed to publicly post results on Thursday. KYW news time is 7:40 —"

Switching channels.

"Can they still lay me off even though I'm on disability?"

"Yes, and they should! I'll say it again: you are not protected from being laid off!"

Change the station.

"I want to get these documents sent from Orange County to another state and — "

"Look Heather, if you had been dealing with my company, I would have gotten on the phone during the next commercial break and started screaming at them at the top of my lungs, and I'd get them to act. Believe it. But look what happens when you go to ACME Tax Company: you get screwed over! Tell them to get on the stick *now*, and I mean *now*, or you'll file an instant lawsuit —"

Flip again and the dashboard picks up a guy yelling somewhere down in Florida: "Great, folks! Big oil has to play this ridiculous 'green game' and now they're getting sued for it! After causing starvation problems around the world, we're learning that home owners in Florida are reporting problems with their lawn equipment —"

Switch.

"We saw the carnage on our television sets and on the internet. Does that feed into what the terrorists are doing, this availability to the media? We're here at the Green Acres mall in Valley Stream—"

One nice thing about driving alone from city to city is that I can wear the same outfit every day and nobody knows.

Work

What does it mean to be a man? A man has insurance, stock options, an investment portfolio, a dentist, mutual funds, and knowledge of his blood pressure. I don't have any of these things, although I do own a pair of cuff links that I keep on my dresser. I never wear them, yet they impart a protective power: the image of a company man with a dental plan and a definite hairstyle.

My Grandfather. Radar operator in World War II. Thirty-eight years at Sears, Roebuck & Co. Retired in 1982 and served as township supervisor of Caseville, Michigan, until moving to Florida in 2000 and an assisted living facility back in Michigan in 2007.

My Father. Explosive Ordnance Disposal during the Vietnam War, stationed in Korea. Ten years at Sears, Roebuck & Co. before the division that he managed was outsourced to China in 1984. A brief stint in two pyramid schemes for selling fire extinguishers and bathroom supplies. Various retail positions for companies such as Children's Palace, Office Max, and Home Goods.

Me. Hedge clipper at ATCO Precision Tool, busboy at Heartland restaurant, sales clerk in the electrical department at Sears, Roebuck & Co., barista at Caribou Coffee, sales clerk at Service Merchandise, office assistant at the Center for Japanese Studies, office assistant at Stucky Vitale Architects, cashier at a liquor store, clerk at an oriental rug store, waiter at a French bistro, waiter at an Indian restaurant, photo technician at CPI Photo, sales clerk at the jewelry counter of JC Penney, photo technician at Ritz Photo, technical assistant at the University of Michigan department of Film and Video, clerk at Amoco gas station, various pizza delivery gigs, multimedia consultant at the University of Michigan Media Union, preparing graphics for civil litigation, partner in a record label, techno deejay and music producer, teaching assistant at the High School for Communication Arts, program director of the Pratt Summer Design School, adjunct faculty at Pratt Institute, visiting faculty at Parsons School of Design, founder and creative director of a design studio called Red Antenna, writer of a blog called Big American Night, partner in a company called Civic Center, considering law school.

Old Industry Overwhelms Me. I drive past brick factories with faded letters, painted back when signs were handmade and mentioned the owner's sons. Milling and punching shops. Silos and precision drilling. Aluminum Window Guard Co. and Combustion Servicing Inc. Cho Yang shipping containers. Maersk. Cho Yang. Sealand. Piles of car parts. Rusted trains and broken docks framed by mountains of gravel and scrap iron. Big machines rotting in the American sun. They say we're living in the digital age, yet we're left with the corpses of the last one.

So many towns with shuttered main streets, overgrown factories, and the husks of empty silos. *We used to make things*. A haunting refrain. They say when America loses a manufacturing job, it never comes back. Nonetheless, some men keep building things. They keep lifting and loading and fastening and hauling. With my laptop I feel like a little boy playing at work.

Sears. Soon after he retired, my grandfather moved back to the house on the lake in Caseville, where he was elected township supervisor because, as he put it, he needed something to do after putting in thirty-eight years at Sears. Thirty-eight years working for one company. I can't imagine it. But Sears was very good to him. He started out doing basic sales stuff in Kalamazoo but, thanks to the GI Bill, he quickly made assistant manager because he had a degree from the University of Michigan.

In 1963, he was promoted and he moved his family to Chicago, where he did promotions for the repair department, starting out in regional and moving up to the national office. When his wife got cancer ten years later, Sears pulled him off the road and put him in Home Improvement. "Department 26," my dad remembers. "He worked with washers and dryers, developing new products. When Whirlpool came out with the first combination washer and dryer, my mom hated it. It took ages to do a load of laundry. He was still there when I got promoted from Grand Rapids to Chicago. He worked on the tenth floor and I was on the twelfth."

And how did my father end up at Sears? "I was thinking about medical school because my mom forced it down my throat," he says. "But I didn't have much ambition at the time. I'd have been better off going into the military right after graduation. I was seventeen. I wasn't mature enough to think about a career. But instead of the military, I went straight to college and majored in business. Even going to work for a year or two, I'd have been much better off." He gets quiet and I think about my undergraduate years: the bad poetry and booze, the laziness and confusion — and, worst of all, the sense of entitlement. I definitely could have used a year or two of hard labor after high school. Maybe five. Strange to hear my father say the same thing.

I worked at Sears, too. It wasn't a conscious decision: I went to the local mall when I was sixteen and Sears was hiring. They put me in the lighting department where I sold night-lights and ceiling fans for two months before quitting to work in a coffee shop, which also lasted only a few weeks. This became a pattern.

My father expected to work at Sears for a long time. "Sears took good care of me for thirteen years," he says, "but like most big companies at the time, they changed. Downsizing and offshoring. Three thousand layoffs, including me. I took a job with a manufacturer who went bankrupt three years later. Now I'm working for peanuts and trying to find a good full-time position with a decent company. It's hard. You just don't find it anymore."

Profession. No matter the city, I'll sit in the bar around five o'clock and watch the same scene with jealousy: men drinking beer and laughing, slapping shoulders and looking like they own the place. They wear ironic t-shirts, designer jeans, and expensive sneakers. Or maybe they wear suits and their neckties are loose. Or maybe their work gloves and plastic helmets are piled on the table. These men know what they're about. They belong to a world with its own logic, slang, and rules.

I've never stuck with anything long enough to feel this way. The trouble comes in choosing one thing. I want to do everything. But we think in the singular: *What do you want to be when you grow up? Pick one.* I've had twenty-nine jobs. I've rolled Persian carpets and served crêpes and illustrated jet-ski engines for courtroom presentations. I've taught kindergarten and high school and I stopped teaching because the pay was lousy and there was no autonomy. I'm ashamed to admit that. I don't think I should make more money building websites than teaching your kids. But I do.

Labor. Riding the F train to Coney Island on a cold morning, I glimpse a red car pulling out of a driveway. Thick exhaust billows under sodium lights. I flash on being small. Seven or eight years old. My mom gently shakes me awake, apologizing. Still dark outside. Coffee percolates and the radio murmurs from the kitchen. The Pontiac idles in the driveway, warming up. Frost spiders across the windshield and stuffy heat blasts out of the vents while I twist in the backseat and try to fall asleep again.

We had only one car, and my parents needed to get to their jobs on opposite sides of the city and I needed to be dropped at school. I slept in the back. After dropping off my dad for his six o'clock shift, I climbed into the front seat where a cold sunrise blushed against the dark while we drive forty miles back downtown. We flipped from News Radio 950 to the Morning Zoo. Aretha Franklin's "Freeway of Love" was always playing. So was "Who's Zoomin' Who." Detroit loved Aretha. My mom and I loved Aretha. We sang along and I jabbered away until she dropped me off at school and went to her accounting job.

When I think of discipline, I think of that cold car warming up in the driveway: my dad waking up at five in the morning six days a week on those dead winter mornings. When I can't sleep, sometimes I ride the train. My sleep patterns are elastic. I occasionally teach a class or appear at a meeting, but for the most part I keep my own schedule. Sometimes I rent an office, other times I work from home. I've always got a zillion half-cocked projects in the queue and if I get wound too tight and overcaffeinated I'll find myself riding the train at three or four in the morning, those in-between hours when, sure, you've got the drunk, the homeless, and the confused, but also sturdy guys working night shifts, double shifts, and swing shifts. Carhartt and wool caps and serious boots. These men are younger than me, yet they seem much older. They have wedding bands and kids. They probably pay their bills on time. They probably know exactly what to do if their car starts making a clunking sound. I feel like a child. I live in an imaginary world. I make virtual things.

I feel spoiled. I use this word in the most literal sense. *Ruined.* I worry that I'm incapable of discipline. I fear that I'm soft. How did I end up here? How did that guy wind up sweeping the subway platform at four in the morning?

On the early morning train, I watch that red car pull out of the driveway, exhaust billowing in the cold, some sleepy guy heading to the office. I stetch and stare at the subway advertisements. I'm startled by all of the 1-800 numbers for life's catastrophes: 1-800-INNOCENT. 1-800-DIVORCE. Don't Let Impotence Ruin Your Sex Life: 1-800-866-MALE. Gorgeous Skin: 1-800-BLEMISH. Break Free: 1-800-BANKRUPT. Shockwave Treatment for Chronic Heel Pain! Change Your Life, Get a New Job Parking Cars in Manhattan! And there's an ad for a thriller novel: *At a remote Tibetan monastery, something unholy has begun . . . and only Pendergast can stop it!*

I lean against the scratched-up subway window, watching the cars making their way to the Brooklyn Queens Expressway, getting a jump on the morning commute. The sky lightens. I want to be Pendergast. I want a life of adventure.

Notes on a 2001 Interview for a Production Artist Position. After an exhausting interrogation of my computer skills, the round man at the big advertising agency adjusts his rimless glasses and sighs. He runs his fingers across the dozens of other résumés fanned across the conference table. He smiles. He's shopping for production artists and he enjoys it. This is my first interview in New York and I'm a nervous mess. He sighs again, stretching things out.

"So you know the software," he says at last, "but what do you really want to do?"

"At this company? Or in general?"

He leans forward and flashes that unnerving smile. "In general."

I beat back the fun responses like "Find Christ" or "Live in the jungle with nothing more than a sharpened stick and my wits." The best thing to do is answer honestly, but what I want to do has nothing to do with pushing pixels for this gray company. I want to make big important gestures. I want adventure. I want to get wild and walk away from a burning car. I want to get political. I want to publish a novel. I want to write a novel. I want to come home one day and surprise my lady friend with tickets to Monte Carlo. I want the president of the United States to ask me to assassinate somebody or recover a precious jewel and then I'll gravely hold up a hand and tell him I'm retired. For good.

I want to know that everything's going to be okay for everybody that I know. To be assured that there is life after death, that somebody's been in charge all along and there's a good explanation for things like sadists, bullets, saxophone solos, and teal. I want to find my old Legos and I want to be big and strong and take up lots of space. Someday I'd like to hear somebody call me a pillar of the community. I'd like to have a pot of geraniums that I'll water every morning and sometimes I'll make small talk with my neighbor, a wizened old man who is cranky and despondent at first but soon proves to be intriguing and full of secrets. I'll endear myself to him and he'll invite me over for chess and teach me valuable life lessons.

I want to have fantasies that don't come from the movies.

Finally I answer: "I want to be a good worker."

I didn't get the job.

Interview. The second plane hit Tower 2 three hours ago. We stood in the middle of Sixth Avenue watching the buildings collapse. We gaped at the showers of paperwork and the rolling gray clouds. We covered our mouths. Some of us got phone calls and crumpled to the pavement. The streets were too heavy. I retreated to the rooftop and watched everything fall apart.

I'd been in New York for six weeks and I still didn't have a job. But I had an interview in an hour. The prospect of being a functioning citizen in the big city seemed like a pipe dream — and this interview, to scan newspaper advertisements for nine bucks an hour, felt like a big deal. Hell was coming down everywhere and I was worried about this interview. Did they still expect me to go? Should I call? In the face of shock, I micromanage. Maybe we all do.

I picked up the phone and dialed: "Hello? I have an interview at 11:30 and . . . yeah, right. I'm not going to make it because of the . . ."

"Right." The man on the other end understood. "We don't know what's going on today. Shall we reschedule?"

We checked our calendars and scheduled a time for next week as if nothing were out of the ordinary. I got the job. I scanned toothpaste and shampoo advertisements into a database. I quit ten days later.

Bellhop. I once worked as a bellhop in a hotel that was attached to a hospital. People came to wait and worry and mourn. The hours were good and there wasn't much bellhopping to do. I learned one thing: when you're pushing somebody in a wheelchair, always walk backward into the elevator so the person is facing the door rather than the back wall. I didn't catch on to this until an old lady yelled at me for "parking her like a piece of goddamned furniture." Those words still ring in my head today, mixed metaphor and all.

I eventually got fired for smoking cigarettes and watching TV in the guest rooms. They caught me when I set off the smoke alarm. We had to evacuate everybody in the building, but even with lights flashing and sirens screaming I remembered to point the wheelchairs toward the elevator door.

The Lousy Model. I'm drawing a naked man. *Sketch him out fast, fast!* The slope of his forehead, the cylinder of his neck, his arms, and then go around his chest and down his back and, yes, his genitals, too. His *organ*, she calls it. Now draw him quick, quick! The teacher stands behind me, snapping her fingers. "The entire body should be done by now, but you're still working on his head!"

"He looks so sad."

"Just get the form. We're looking for volume here, not expression."

The model is in his late fifties, bald and sickly looking. Five-nine, one twenty at best. He has no volume and he looks absolutely dejected. He stares into the portable space heater, fighting back tears. I thought nude models were supposed to be pretty and round and bouncy with full lips and an exhibitionistic glint.

"One minute left! Work fast, fast!" She claps her hands. Then she grabs my pencil. "Here, round out his buttocks to get the musculature."

Is she blind? The man's a stick. A sad and depressing stick that has no buttocks, let alone musculature.

"Time's up!" She claps again. The model lunges for his robe and wraps it around his stick body while easels creak and sketch pads rustle. He stands in the back of the studio near the pencil sharpener with his head down while she criticizes and praises. His wet rabbit eyes blink fast and dart around the floor. Not once does he look up to see the twenty-one drawings of his skinny arms and sagging chest.

"Now we'll do a thirty-minute pose," she says. His head snaps up and I swear he's on the edge of tears as he drops the blue terry-cloth robe and sits in the center of the room, adjusting the space heater for maximum comfort.

"Okay, work quick, quick! Be sure to get the folds and creases this time!"

He tilts his chin high and blinks hard. He's staring at the clock.

Things I learned after meeting with a pharmaceutical company. You cannot show anybody climbing or running in advertisements for medication because this might imply that the product will give consumers the ability to climb mountains or run a race when, in fact, it does not. For this reason, showing a person standing on a high porch with stairs or a hilltop is frowned upon. Also, you cannot depict more than three people in a festive setting or at a social gathering such as a barbecue because this could be interpreted as an activity that may lead to an orgy.

Protect Your Device. A paranoid subway poster from the NYPD says: *Earphones are a giveaway. Protect your device!* Everybody has a device nowadays. All of the pretty girls are plugged in, the lonely men stare at tiny films, and important people punch endless numbers on impossible keyboards; everyone else stares spellbound into their telephones. People nod to music that I cannot hear and type things that I cannot see. I have no idea what everyone is up to behind their little screens.

Trains are better when the only diversion is the page. Let's all read newspapers and listen to the gray rush and grind of the train, let's make obvious comments about delays or the temperature and roll our eyes at the baffling performances of the crazy and entrepreneurial. Books and newspapers and magazines may create private spaces, too, but at least I can see the covers: the *New York Post* or Marcel Proust. I can judge you.

Art Girl. She wore a t-shirt that said "Self-Service" in big block letters and had a dog named Peter Jennings. When she mentioned that she was in an art show, I decided to stop by and say hello. Her art was big and intimidating: enormous car doors covered in glitter and she made it worse by talking about framing, reference, and the integrity of the picture plane. I stepped outside, plotting an escape. A man with paint-splattered jeans paced and growled. "So for her final presentation she does this performance piece where she induces vomiting. Four times. In a cup." He flicked his cigarette into the street. "Fucking art students."

Hearst Castle. We stood blinking in the courtyard of the famous castle on top of San Simeon, dazzled by the marble statues, orange groves, and palm trees. We gawked at the zebras, tennis courts, and swimming pools. "Unlike most of us, Mr. William Randolph Hearst was able to make his dreams come true." Our tour guide said this and it set the tone for an incredibly depressing hour.

Garbage. Thundering toward the Confusion Range, I race past Utah's red rocks and yellow ridges and take a hard left on a dirt road just off Route 50, kicking up clouds of dust and snaking through canyons of old tires and mountains of twisted rebar and rusted chrome. A handwritten sign says *Dumping Zone.* An ancient man at the checkpoint waves me through without looking up.

I drive along a road of packed garbage, picking my way through a stinky patch of American hell: busted baby carriages, chicken bones, refrigerator doors, blue jeans, beer cans, shredded tires . . . all of it shimmering beneath the hundred-degree desert sun. The smell kicks me in the guts and, when I step out of the car to double over, a bulldozer revs to life.

I wave at the bulldozer and the driver cuts the engine. He tells me the usual landfill story. It's filling up too fast and now they're paying inmates from the county jail forty dollars a day to pick up the stray garbage. The landfill gets covered once a week. "But we can't keep pace anymore and I don't know how to keep up. I'm not a city boy — this is my office and it's getting too danged crowded."

Blue Station. I worked the late shift at a gas station. This was back in the blurry years between 96 and 99. There was a nightly AA meeting around the corner. I went once or twice but it wasn't for me. I worked the late shift at the Amoco and tried to keep busy instead. Every night after the meeting let out, an old-timer would come in, glance at the empty coffee pot next to the beer cooler and ask if I planned to make any coffee that night. He had anxious eyes and wore an old satin windbreaker and always looked like he was cold.

Making coffee was one of my few duties as a gas station clerk but I didn't drink coffee yet so I didn't appreciate its import or know how to make it. Besides, I was too busy chain-smoking Kools and staring out the window and writing terrible poetry. Really bad stuff that I actually set fire to a few years later. So nobody who came to the Amoco had any coffee and if they did, it was from some cold pot set out earlier in the afternoon. A few customers offered to make it themselves but I didn't know where the materials were kept. I was a bastard back then and sometimes I wish I could find that sad guy in the windbreaker, apologize, and make him an amazing pot of fancy coffee.

Retail creep. Whenever my father mentions his work schedule to my grandfather, there is confusion.

"Why are you calling so late?"

"My store doesn't close until ten, Dad."

In my grandfather's day, stores were open five days a week, nine to five, with special evening hours on Wednesday. Today most stores keep their doors open seven days a week for twelve or thirteen hours at a stretch. During the holidays, they might open at six in the morning and close at midnight. Sometimes they stay open all the time.

"But they pay you overtime for working that late, don't they?"

"No."

Imagine if in 1975 a company announced that starting tomorrow, most full-time positions would be replaced with part-time shifts paid at a reduced hourly wage. Imagine if the store also announced that it was busting its unions, forcing its remaining full time employees to pay more for less health coverage, and exponentially increasing the salaries of its top management, most of whom will now operate out of a remote office in Delaware where they will manage a variety of unrelated companies and spectral investments. There'd probably be a riot. But these changes happened in drips and drabs and nowadays people are accustomed to working more for less. And that's why every time my father calls his father, he must remind him why he's getting up at five in the morning tomorrow or not getting home until eleven at night.

Dinosaur Tracks. When I see the sign for dinosaur tracks I hit the brakes. As soon as I step out of the car, a gigantic Navajo man named Todd takes my arm and pulls me through a breakneck tour of Stego-saurus tracks, a possible Triceratops battle, and maybe a T. Rex nest. A few of the footprints resemble monster chicken feet, but most of them look like random grooves scratched into the hard red mud. "See here?" he says, poking at the ground with a stick. "You can tell there was a lot of activity by these ridges."

I'm more interested in the logistics of Todd's business. He points to his home in the distance, set among a cluster of tough-looking aluminum shacks backed against a cliff. Todd and his brother have spent years combing the area for tracks and putting up signs so they can show them to people like me. Entrepreneurship in its purest form.

"There's a fantastic set of raptor prints behind that ridge," he says.

"How much do I owe you so far?"

"Oh, there's no charge. I'm just happy to share the history of my land with you. Donations are appreciated, though."

I give him a five-dollar bill and he frowns. "You're not happy with what you've seen?"

"It's all I have."

He takes it and walks away without a word.

Shoeshine. I'm sitting on a bench along the Mississippi River in New Orleans, thinking about where to go next, when a spindly old man in a filthy linen suit stops and says, "Nice shoes! I'll bet I can guess the city where you got 'em." I wave him off but he keeps pushing. "C'mon man, don't treat me like a bum! I'm sixty-three years old and I'm proposing a gentleman's wager. If I can guess the city where you got your shoes, you let me shine 'em. Hell, I'll even tell you what *street* you got 'em on." He snaps a rag and grins.

Okay, I'll bite. He leans close. "You got your shoes on your feet right here on Decatur Street in New Orleans. Right? *Am I right?*"

"Well played."

Now he's shining my shoes and I feel awful about it. One of the oldest cons in history, and I fell for it. He chatters and shines away while I look around, embarrassed, wondering if I have any money and how much I should give him. "Don't be so anxious to go," he says. "Let me do these right." When he's finished, he tells me that it'll be eight dollars per shoe.

"No way!"

"You're a sore loser."

I pull out a wad of singles. "Here's four bucks."

"All right, just gimme twelve. I'm doing you a favor."

"I'm doing you a favor. You did a terrible job shining my shoes, but I admire your racket, so here's four bucks. Take it or don't."

He grabs it and calls me a sore loser again. He tells his friends I owe him money.

Strange Men in the Bathroom. There are strange men in the bathroom of my office building. Two guys sometimes speak in hushed conspiratorial tones with piles of paperwork balanced on the sink. When I enter, they look up and say "Please come in" as if inviting me into their home.

One day the sink was filled with hair. Lots of it. This wasn't just a shave, it was a fugitive on the run frantically fumbling with scissors and hair dye. Another time I was greeted by a man planted in the middle of the room and wearing only boxers. He gave me a cheery wave before disappearing into a stall and making a lot of noise. There's another guy you sometimes catch washing his feet in the sink with his socks draped over the paper towel dispenser. And the young man who brushes his teeth like a maniac: he keeps his arm perfectly still while jerking his head against the toothbrush like a piston. It's terrifying to watch.

And there's the guy who conducts important business on his phone while peeing. One time he was saying "Yes, thanks for following up — we're reviewing several applications and we'll be in touch soon." I flushed and he flashed me the dirtiest look, as if I were the inconsiderate one.

These things happen and yet when we pass each other in the hall or stand together in the elevator we act as if everything is normal.

Bad Words. One nice thing about being a designer and a teacher is that I get to work with a lot of different people and organizations, from big corporations and professors to city bureaucrats and obscure nonprofit groups. In the process, I've discovered there are several words that make me completely shut down as soon as I hear them. Here they are, all at once: Assessment. Mortgage. Financing. 401K. Coverage. Media. Ratio. Ontological. Inflation. Investment. Signifier. Organic. Annuity. Environmentalism. Interest rate. Arbitrage. Jurisdiction. Interdisciplinary. Dividend. Co-payment. NASDAQ. Deduction. Budget. Assets. User. Carbon. Equity. Click-through. Usability. Liability. Crowdsourcing. Analytics. Medicaid. Insurance. Flowchart. APR. Proliferation. Emissions. Subsidized. Reflexive. Consumer culture. Whole grain. Subprime. Cardiovascular. Antioxidant. Fiscal. Semiotics. Fiber. Social responsibility. Bond. Capital. Networking. Sustainable. Salad.

... get and ...

... NAA. THE IDEA ... like a play ...

... sorro ... advertisements for ... and I picked

review of 11:3 ...

My Handwriting Is Shit. This was originally written in longhand. Just a Uni-ball Vision .5mm black ink pen and a Moleskine notebook. Frustrated by the squiggly auto-corrections of Microsoft Word and the distractions of the world wide web, I write almost everything by hand. My notebook bursts with page after page of choppy, bunched-up scribblings that I can barely decipher. It's the demented notebook that the detectives uncover while searching the serial killer's basement.

I want the crisp and confident handwriting found on an international postcard circa 1922: a smart script cocked at a jaunty angle, bursting with generous loops and buxom flourishes that conjure passionate love affairs and brilliant manuscripts. Flipping through my grandparents' wartime letters, my heart floods with envy. I could never create anything so classy. I have the penmanship of a spastic penguin: tight and jittery, without a shred of dignity.

Everything I learned from my kindergarten cursive worksheets has atrophied. In high school, I should have refined my penmanship through the writing of countless book reports and social studies papers — but that's when the computer came on the scene along with the sentence that changed everything: *In a 3-5 page TYPED essay* . . . Teachers would no longer suffer the panicked scratchings of harried teenagers (who could blame them?). Now my handwriting can be carbon dated to the year when Microsoft Word reached critical mass.

I am doomed to live with the introverted scrawl of a nervous thirteen-year-old. When it comes to penmanship, most of my generation is also stuck in 1990. Whenever I see someone under forty writing in cursive, it is cause for comment — along with a strange mixture of admiration, suspicion, and jealousy.

At what point will handwriting no longer be required? Does it matter if our penmanship deteriorates? I'm at a loss for scenarios in which handwriting is a necessity, aside from a half assed signature for the UPS guy or a few garbled digits on a government form.

The only benefit is esteem. Staring at my inky mess, my sixth-grade teacher comes to mind. Mrs. Drexel. I'm eleven years old and standing at the blackboard, diagramming a sentence about the location of an imaginary aunt's imaginary houseplant. I step back from my work and wait for Mrs. Drexel's judgment: did I successfully locate the gerund? Her permanent scowl becomes a pinched little nightmare as she accelerates toward the chalkboard, her giant plastic glasses raised before her like a windshield.

"Good Lord, Jimmy! Your handwriting is absolutely awful." She leans in close to the board, raising and lowering her glasses. "Look at it. So small and bunched together." She turns to the class. "You know what it means when someone writes like this? It means they're insecure." And that was the day I started feeling insecure.

Chaos Theory & the Bell

Today is my first day in a classroom and I'm worried. I don't know what to expect. I take comfort in my designation as a "Non-Participant Observer." Small children mystify me. I consider making a big name tag that emphasizes my non-participant status.

I.

After making my way past the security guard, I find the art room. Ms. Bannister and I shake hands. "So you want to be a teacher, huh?" She laughs and returns to her paperwork. I hear a rumbling outside the door. A rowdy clamor grows louder. I want to run.

Twenty-three first-graders burst through the door and gather on the dirty carpet. They smell like Velveeta. Lindsay announces that she has a bleeding tooth, which sends shock waves through the class. Sympathy flows. The children take turns recounting their dental war stories

Aaron raises his hand. "Guess what everybody?"

"What?"

"I lost two teeth last month."

Murmurs of approval.

"And you know what else? I played baseball until eight o'clock last night."

Now everybody's talking.

"I like pink."

"There was blood everywhere."

"I bought some glue."

"Red's okay, too."

"I don't go to the dentist."

"Are you married?"

Ms. Bannister shushes them. She critiques their popsciple-stick picture frames. I drift. I can't believe the madness that parents let their kids wear. There's a seven-year-old girl in a vinyl camouflage bodysuit and two boys who have never had a haircut. They wear wife-beaters. Maybe they're in a band.

The kids march to three big tables. Two crazy boys run around in tight little circles, chanting "boxers." Ms. Bannister doesn't say anything. She sets out a box of fabric scraps and the kids go apeshit slicing up paisley, checker, gingham, and houndstooth. They love the gingham. They chop away with the dullest scissors ever manufactured. A small boy named Sam tugs on my sleeve. "Can you cut this for me?" He doesn't grasp the concept of a "non-participant" observer. I squeeze my fingers through his plastic scissors. The gingham refuses to yield and I don't know what to tell him. I give him back the fabric and scissors. "Good luck with that."

A boy douses his paper with glue, quietly chanting "I hate freedom, I hate freedom" in a dead monotone. Nobody notices. The kids who were shouting "boxers" now chant "wide load" as they run around a large girl.

Cleanup time. When Ms. Bannister sees a big sticky clump of glue on the table, she demands an explanation from the freedom-hating boy, who denies it. Ms. Bannister does everything short of calling him a liar before giving up. She escorts the students to the cafeteria. Two girls linger behind. "You wanna hear a song?" Before I can decline, they're singing, "I love freedom, I love freeeeeedom" over and over and I begin to think that creepy boy was on to something.

When Ms. Bannister returns to the empty classroom she looks beaten. "They're so whacked out," she says. "I just try to keep them in a holding pattern as long as I can." She tells a story: something bad happened to one of her students in a public bathroom, so the girl's parents told her that she was only allowed to use the bathroom at home. They sent their daughter to school in diapers. When the girl had to go, she raced around the classroom shrieking. She wasn't about to use the diapers. She was trapped. Sometimes she tried to use the sink. This went on for weeks, and —

The next class arrives. Ms. Bannister never finishes the story. I'm filled with questions but I don't ask; it's a weird thing to take an interest in.

II.

When I arrive the next day, they wave and grin. "Hooray, James is back!" Two of the kids hug me. I'm unprepared for this. I think they're mocking me.

The mood on the carpet is heavy. Somebody was "roaring" in the hallway and Ms. Bannister is determined to flush out the culprit. "A lot of people won't admit when they do something wrong because they're afraid of getting punished," she says. "What do you think?"

A tiny girl with a ladybug on her shirt raises her hand. "Well, if you do something bad and don't tell, you'll have to live with it for the rest of your life."

A boy throws up his hand, too. "And . . . and sometimes you worry about it but you don't get punished at all, so it's better to tell instead of punishing yourself." So young, yet these kids are already well versed in the mechanics of guilt and anguish. Maybe it'll come through in their art.

Ms. Bannister smiles. "Good. If you want to come up to my desk and privately tell me that you were the one roaring, I won't punish you and I'm sure we'll both feel better."

Roaring in the hall is evil, but running in circles around a girl and chanting "wide load" goes unpunished? I shouldn't judge. I wasn't here for the roaring. Maybe it was really loud.

While the students work on their popsicle-stick frames, Ms. Bannister walks among the tables and helps them cut the impossible gingham. She points out Emily's frame. "Everybody stop and look at Emily's frame," she says. "There are nice things about everybody's frames, but Emily's is particularly nice because she stayed in the same color family. She used purple ink, pink paper, and pink and purple beads." The kids stare at Ms. Bannister. Emily sways proudly.

"Is purple a primary color?" asks Ms. Bannister. Some say yes, some say no. Work resumes.

When Ms. Bannister wants the class's attention, she calls out "Class!" or sometimes "Everyone!" This usually works well enough, although mumbling and running still persist. When absolute 100 percent undivided attention is required she rings a bell. One of those old silver bells found at courtesy desks and old motels. This bell has power. The children fall dead silent for the bell, as if it once brutally attacked them.

Ms. Bannister rings the bell. Chatter stops cold. She uses this rare silence to congratulate the four students who've finished their frames. She asks them to help those still working. They mill around. They stare at me. Emily patrols the tables, shoving her glorified purple frame in everybody's face. The other kids hate her.

Sam, the little boy who likes me, asks me to draw him something. I'm not sure why he likes me, since I failed to cut his gingham.

"I can't draw," I say.

"Anything. Just do it. *Now.*"

He yanks the pen from my hand and gives me an orange marker. "Tiger orange is the best color ever," he says. (He's wrong. Mint green is the best color ever.) I draw a robot and it's terrible. He grabs the paper and scurries off. I worry. He hates it, I'm sure. I should have spent more time. Maybe given it a nice shadow. Or at least defined the chrome.

III.

Ms. Bannister discusses the project for the week: they're midway through making masks. Because class periods are so short (often only 45 minutes, which is the state minimum), long-term projects maximize class time: less time is spent giving instructions and there's no rush to immediately finish.

The kids scamper to the tables, mobbing and shouldering one another to get at the best brushes and felts. Eventually, they settle down with their work: a cartoon sea of oranges, pinks, and greens strung together with Elmer's glue. Judging from the bright colors and angular shapes, there's a distinct African influence in their masks. Ms. Bannister says they've been studying "forced immigration, particularly the slavery of Africa." I nod politely. Two girls quietly glue beads to their cheeks. One of them has a spike and wears a t-shirt that says "Meat Sauce."

Ms. Bannister moves among the three long tables, spending a few minutes with each student. A girl sits before a beautiful disaster of every single color and shade of glitter.

She looks perplexed. Ms. Bannister leans over and talks about "visual unity." "You don't need to do everything at the same time," she says.

Another girl refuses to work. She's been staring at the door for about fifteen minutes. Ms. Bannister tells her to start working or go sit on the carpet. The angry girl never says a word or nods or anything. She just stares back coldly. You can tell she hates Ms. Bannister.

"Maybe you need to go to the nurse?"

The girl glares harder. She gets up and leaves, slamming the door.

The students return to the dirty carpet, where Ms. Bannister reviews the day's progress. Sam's banner is bright orange with his name in yellow felt. He wears an orange hat and a yellow shirt. His sneakers are orange. I see a yellow and orange backpack hanging on the wall. This kid could teach Little Miss Glitter a thing or two about visual unity.

Angry Girl returns and sits on the edge of the group, her back turned to everybody. Ms. Bannister notices but says nothing (I think she's afraid of Angry Girl). Everything she says is punctuated with a misbehaving student's name. "So we could use wood or thread — ASHLEY! — or paint — SAM!"

IV.

The following morning, the class gathers on the dirty rug to await instructions. They're going to make calendars this week. Ms. Bannister quizzes them about what makes for a good illustration.

"Drawings of me in Puerto Rico."

"My friends."

"No, *my* friends."

"Pictures of my dog standing on my bed."

She refuses to call on one kid. "I'm not going to call on squeaky people," she says. It's ninety degrees outside and there's no air-conditioning. The children are restless, squirming and wheezing, sighing and staring at the ceiling. One boy does all of these things at once. "Max," says Ms. Bannister, "I'm going to have you sit here for five minutes while the rest of the class works. You can practice sitting still."

The kids shout and argue while drawing snowmen, witches, and birthday cakes. As Ms. Bannister helps them draw, I notice she moves the marker like a trained artist, working gracefully from the arm, not the wrist.

A boy tugs on my sleeve. "This is a drawing of me when I got locked up." He's sketched a little red figure smothered in a dense grid of blue. It's frightening, like something that would be used in an advertisement for antidepressants. The girl sitting across from him is drawing a fine kite. Sharp and clear, it belongs in a library of clip art.

Max sobs quietly at his desk, his face buried in his arms, surrounded by crumpled paper. "I keep messing up! It's terrible!" Somebody should show him the crap the other kids have turned in, but nobody approaches him. I consider becoming a participant observer. If Ms. Bannister is aware of Max's angst, she doesn't show it. Maybe he does this all the time. But if she just rescued one of his crumpled drawings, wouldn't he suddenly be filled with pride? I do it. I uncrumple a demented-looking snowman and tell him it's not so bad, that it's pretty good actually. He beams and I feel like a hero for the rest of the day.

Ms. Bannister reviews the calendar assignment, using the opportunity to teach them about themes. "What are the seasons of the year?" she asks.

"Months!"

"Leaves!"

She shuts her eyes and looks zen. "What goes in the same category as spring?"

"Fall."

"And?"

"Autumn!"

"It's the same thing. What else?"

"Winter?"

"Good. And one more . . ."

Silence.

"Okay. Spring, winter, fall, and — why is it so hot?"

"Summer!"

"Great, and what are these things called? Sam?"

Sam stares at the ceiling. "Seams."

"Anyone else?"

A long silence and then a girl hisses, "Seasons."

Ms. Bannister goes over this a few more times, along with the concept of holidays.

They continue drawing their calendar pictures. A boy worries about finishing too early. "What happens then?" Ms. Bannister tells him that he can do whatever he wants. He begins working very slowly.

At the end of class they return to the carpet, where Ms. Bannister has collected their pictures. She holds up a page with a stick figure witch and a pumpkin. "Is this a season or a holiday?"

Silence. It's truth time. Did they retain anything from thirty-five minutes ago?

"It's a drawing of a jack-o'-lantern, right?"

The kids agree to this.

"So what's the theme?"

"October!"

Painful.

"No. We spent a lot of time talking about this — is it a season or a . . ."

"Holiday!"

The bell rings.

"Just in time." Ms. Bannister sinks back into her chair.

It's hot again. They're cranky. Ms. Bannister discusses the calendar project that the other classes have been working on. I'm sick of the calendar project. I wonder if she is, too.

She asks them how many months are in a year. Silence. "Okay then, let's name them — all together now." They do it perfectly, which is reassuring.

Another teacher comes in. "Wow, this room is much cooler," she says. The students anxiously raise their hands, eager to inform her about the science behind the cool temperature.

"It's because we're underground."

"We don't get any sun."

"This used to be the teacher's lunchroom."

The visiting teacher looks wistful. "That right — and it was a long, long time ago."

"The teachers used to be very lucky," says Ms. Bannister.

"It was back when we had money for pencils, paper, and all sorts of supplies."

The two teachers smile at each other.

Ms. Bannister tells the class that she'll be spending the hour preparing for parent-teacher conferences, so today they can make anything they like out of popsicle sticks and glue. This causes one of the kids to freak out. "But what are we making? Tell us!" He doubles over. "I said, what are we making!"

"Whatever you want."

"But we have to make something! Tell us what to do!" He sighs and stares at his shoes.

The kids make what anybody would make with popsicle sticks and glue: they make boxes. Lots of boxes. Four popsicle sticks to form a square, stacked up as high as time and glue will allow. One girl flouts convention and makes a triangle. She MacGyvers some sort of pediment with paper clips and a few Twizzlers. It's the Flatiron Building. It's wild. Everybody mobs around her. They eat her pediment.

At least they're not making ashtrays. I made a gorgeous ashtray in 1985. It looked like an upside-down beehive, painted black with little grooves for your Vantage Lights. My dad used it for a few days and then it held pennies and rubber bands in the laundry room before being retired to the attic. I wonder what will happen to the things these kids make.

Gus waves a popsicle stick in the air and announces his plan to design a building that will hold "everyone in the whole wide world, that way we won't need to use cars anymore." Everybody applauds Gus's eco-friendly vision.

Ms. Bannister assembles the kids' work. She waves a stack of tempura paintings.

"These don't have names, so I need you to tell me if any of this work belongs to you." They riffle through the paintings, puzzled. These kids have no idea if any of the work is theirs or not.

"That's mine."

"You aren't even in my class," says Ms. Bannister. "I think it's Lindsay's."

Lindsay shrugs.

"Didn't you make this? It says 'Mommy kisses me goodnight.'"

"I don't know. Maybe. No."

"I think it's yours."

"Okay."

They fight over Magic Markers. It's vicious. Shouting. Hitting. A valuable lesson in supply and demand. Ms. Bannister sets another coffee can of markers on the table. They continue fighting. Another can of markers is introduced, but it provides little relief. Most of the markers are dried out.

A redheaded girl named Mimi establishes herself as the Marker Commission, claiming all three coffee cans. She tests each marker and doles out the working ones to her comrades. A boy starts a chant of "We want new markers!" and soon the whole table is chanting and pounding the table in unison. It's powerful stuff. They could easily overwhelm Ms. Bannister and take charge of the room — there's strength in numbers and I think they're recognizing this as their chanting becomes more fervent.

The classroom is a disaster. Bits of cardboard, felt, and marker caps litter the floor; kids covered in red tempura, chanting in open revolt, looking like slasher-movie victims; paper scraps everywhere. After the marker drought, they switched to paint. If a grown man could paint with the raw insanity of a five-year-old, he would be hailed as a visionary. Walk into any gallery and you'll see a lot of artists who share this idea.

A boy with a neatly combed helmet of hair paints boxes all over his page. They're elevators, he says. Lots of elevators. He tells Ms. Bannister that he just loves drawing elevators. Elevators are his favorite thing, he says. We nod and walk away.

All of the kids have painted their papers sopping brown and now they're attacking each other with their painty hands. "Everybody quiet!" shouts Ms. Bannister. "Do I need to ring the bell?" Instant silence. How did the bell get so much power? After they clean up, Ms. Bannister directs them to the meeting area, where she's set out some toys. While they play with Lincoln Logs, she collects their paintings and throws them away.

V.

Now they're doing architecture. They've taped together boxes of dog food and cereal and they've covered the boxes with papier-mâché and painted them with tempura. Ms. Bannister asks them to list the architectural elements of a building, which, according to the class, amounts to bricks, doorknobs, and curtains.

A knock at the door. I open it to find a woman gripping the arm of a bohemian child. "This is Mighty Soul and she's arriving late today," says the woman, snapping gum and pushing the little girl forward. Mighty Soul wears a bandanna, a handmade American flag t-shirt, neon green pants, and sandals. She asks if I'm from Australia.

"No. Why do you think that?"

She laughs and runs off. Now I'm self-conscious.

A boy named Fausto tells Mighty Soul that his mom went to jail last month. "She was there for a week and I had to stay with my grandma."

The kids stand on tables with their papier-mâché buildings, jumping around and yelling and smacking one another's work. They leap from chair to chair. A little girl nearly splits her head open. Ms. Bannister is on the other side of the room, gluing windows.

The buildings are ridiculously tall. Four, maybe five feet. These kids are only in first grade and already there's some kind of primal urge driving these buildings higher, into sleek and towering forms. The kids with buildings under four feet tall know they've lost. They work quietly and without passion.

VI.

Today they're working with clay. A girl holds up a gray lump. "I made a ball. I'm done."

Ms. Bannister frowns. "We have thirty minutes left. Maybe you can make something a bit more complex?"

The girl sticks her thumbs in the center of her ball. "Fine. I made a bowl. Or maybe it's a nest. I'm done and I'm going to go wash my hands now."

Ten minutes later, everybody else decides they're done, too, and they bring their work to Ms. Bannister: lazy bowls and half-assed figurines. She doesn't comment on what they've made, she simply tells Mimi to clear out space to store them.

Meanwhile, Fausto staples blank sheets of paper. He's making a book. Max joins him and they spend the rest of class practicing their stapling tactics. They don't make any discernible attempt at writing or drawing anything in their books, although one of the boys gets around to writing "Mega Man X5" on the cover.

Sam stands in front of me, staring and stuffing his fingers into his mouth in unsettling ways. I move to another seat.

"Mimi, would you do me a favor?" asks Ms. Bannister. "Since you were so good at unfolding the tablecloths this morning, could you fold them up for me please?" This girl's gunning to become an administrative assistant.

Ms. Bannister reviews their work: Mega Man, Pokémon, and other licensed characters. Ms. Bannister frowns until a girl named Debbie holds up her drawing. Ms. Bannister beams. "Look everybody! Isn't this nice and original? It's a caterpillar on a leaf!"

"It's Lisa Simpson."

"Of course."

Debbie starts eating her portrait of Lisa Simpson. "Debbie, put it on your lap or I'm going to take it away."

She addresses the class. "It looks like a lot of you are inspired by video games and TV." They nod. She's about to pursue this, but turns back to Debbie: "That's not your lap, that's your mouth."

Class ends.

VII.

"No punching people to take their stuff." This is the first rule of Treasure Chest. Second rule of Treasure Chest: "No punching people to take their stuff." Other than that, it's open season as Ms. Bannister hauls the beat-up suitcase onto Table 2 and pops the top to reveal a hoarder's stash of beads, trinkets, buttons, and other flotsam. The kids swarm, some actually rubbing their hands together in greed. Speculators before a trunk of bullion, imperialists divvying up the world.

They cut shapes from cardboard: shields, swords, medals, and squares. Others string up necklaces, even the boys, although they'll tell you it's for a sister. They tape beads to their ears and glue and color while Ms. Bannister shuffles paperwork.

Jake is determined to make a sword, sheathe, and shield, all gilded with beads and buttons. He has three other students working for him, trafficking beads from the Treasure Chest and coloring his cardboard a darker shade of brown.

I overhear Ms. Bannister talking with another teacher: "Treasure Chest is the ultimate distraction." I imagine reporting this to the students' parents while shaking my head solemnly. *The ultimate distraction.* Would the parents be outraged? Would they care?

The class winds down. Cleanup begins. Ms. Bannister is in a good mood today. Her approach to discipline is sweeter, more rational than usual: "Why do you have a garbage can on your head? Do you think you should be doing that?"

Ms. Bannister tells me not to come in tomorrow. They're showing a movie. "And after that, it's graduation, so I guess this is it."

It's so sudden. I thank her for her time and slip out of the room, suddenly feeling like an intruder. Walking down the stairs, I feel arms around my waist — I spin around to find a little boy. It's Sam. "Thank you for the robot," he says. I make sure he gets down the stairs safely. I'd forgotten about that robot.

AM Radio Scan. Turn the dial to the left as I swing out of New Jersey and a fuzzy blast of Sunday morning gospel music plays: "And I will trust you when your spirit speaks to me, with my whole heart I will agree —"

Flip again. "That's irrelevant! Nobody's going to take care of you! A perfect example is your mortgage —"

Again. "No, no. It's not a class envy argument. I'm not looking for a handout, Ron. I'm just saying that I've done my part, I've earned my pension, and I want to make sure that the auto companies are there to do their part as far as I go. I worked up there in Lordstown and the misconceptions about the people who work there . . . we take so much pride in them cars that come out of there. There's nobody getting paid fifty bucks an hour to put an instruction book in the glove box—"

Change the channel.

"—and so I'm wondering, is it going to get worse? Or should I leave it alone?"

"I think it's safe to say that when you have a problem, it never gets better."

"Right. Just curious."

"It never gets better. The chances are better that it's going to get worse. So I'd go ahead and fix it. The proper way would be to shut off the water, drain the pipes, and cut the pipe right there—"

Plan B: Dial 1-800-USA-TRUCK and start hauling freight across America for eighty-five cents per mile.

Home

What does it mean to be a man? Maybe you need to have a kid. Flipping through old photographs, I see the familiar images of my father splashing and reading and running with me, pictures that formed my memories of being small. But now I'm stunned by the realization that he's younger than me. There he is, twenty-four or twenty-five, suddenly responsible for another person. Man, that'll change your perspective fast — and men keep putting it off: in 1971, the average age for a first-time father was 27. Thirty years later, it was 34.

If I had a kid, I probably wouldn't be driving around right now, brooding and taking pictures of junkyards. Or maybe I'd take him with me.

Overheard in Cheyenne, Wyoming. "Last thing I remember is I was sittin' on the couch waitin' on my wife to get home because, you know, it was wife night . . . and I just remember thinkin' how much I wanted to get the hell away from her and go out drinking. And here I am!"

Overheard in Bartlesville, Oklahoma. "That motherfucker ain't got no home now. He ain't belong to no set now. He can either go uptown and get his ass kicked by them, or he can stay down here and get his ass stomped by me. Either way, that motherfucker's getting his ass beat tonight."

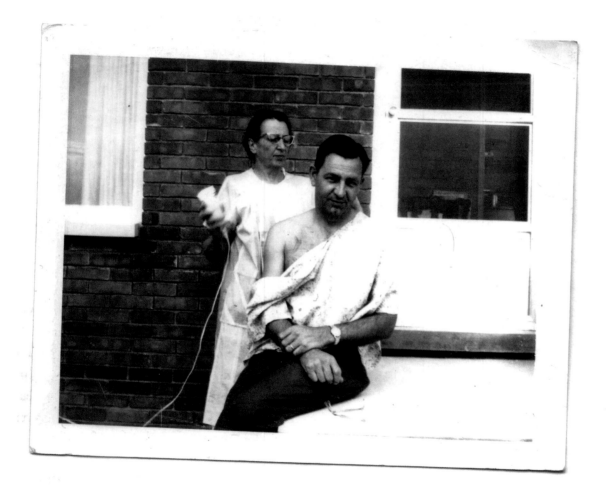

Economy. Even after he returned from the war and got married and became a regional manager, my grandfather would drive two hours from Detroit to Battle Creek to have his mother cut his hair.

At the Lake. "Good morning, Mr. Zip Zip Zip, rise and shine with your hair cut short, your hair cut short like mine. Good morning, Mr. Zip Zip Zip." I wake up to my grandfather singing in a rusty voice while he putters around the house, making instant coffee and starching the day's shirt. He's retired but he dresses up anyway.

Shuffling into the kitchen for coffee, I look at the lake. Gray Michigan waves break across a sandbar. An old tin boat bangs against a twisted aluminum rack with a rusty chain. My great-great-grandfather settled this land. For generations, my family has fished, swum, and retired here. Now it's for sale.

My grandfather quizzes me about what I do for a living in New York. I tell him that I teach and write grants and run a small design studio. He quickly gives up. I don't blame him. I use words like *digital* and *interactive* and I cringe at how vague and fictional my life sounds. I tell him I'm thinking of applying to law school. He gets a kick out of that. I've been saying it for years.

This house on the lake is the only constant in a life spent moving around. Maybe somebody will buy it, perhaps it will be inherited. Either way, I'm pretty sure these are the last days that I will spend here before the property is sold off, probably to be remodeled into a summer rental. Last night I sat on the porch overlooking Saginaw Bay, smoking cigarettes and thinking about law school and taking up running and writing a book and getting healthy. I drank cold coffee and chain smoked. Bonfires burned along the beach and a blast of angry rock echoed across the bay: *take my hand, rock to never neverland.* Dogs barked and screen doors slammed. I'd never seen so many stars. Two cigarettes left in the pack. Rattled. Maybe it's time to leave the country. Maybe it's time to really dig in and commit to something. My parents look old and I don't know what to do about it.

"The word goes down the line, good morning Mr. Zip Zip Zip, you're surely looking fine." My grandfather returns to the ironing board, mumbling through the fragments of some song from a time when women had bulletproof hair and wore long satin gloves and the men drank highballs and joined rotary clubs. An age of cuff links and cars that looked like spacecraft. A time when the milky brass of a distant ballroom band played from enormous wooden radios. An age when a man knew what he had to do. A simpler time, although it probably wasn't.

Army, Part I. "When we got our draft letters, my buddy and I tore a dollar in half. He took one, I took the other, and when we got back together we'd buy a beer with it." My father sits down, raps on the kitchen table, and, in the next ten minutes, he talks to me more than he has in years, telling me about the draft system for Vietnam, about the anxious months he spent waiting to receive his letter, about how nervous he was. "My number was twenty-four, which gave me a good chance of donating two years to Uncle Sam." I quiz him about the details and he keeps talking. Maybe I'm learning to listen. "When my letter arrived in October of 1970," he said, "I appealed it because I only had one month left until graduating from college. I wanted to have my degree before I went to Vietnam."

Vietnam. The name carries such dark weight: chaos, fires, bad acid, napalm, the madness we've seen at the movies. Did my dad know it was going to be crazy? Did he support America's involvement in Vietnam? Did he consider dodging the draft? "Not really, but I didn't understand much of the politics at the time." He gets quiet. "I certainly wasn't *for* the war. But I also knew that if I didn't go, somebody else would go in my place — and so I went."

Iraq. Afghanistan. Iraq again. I try to imagine being drafted into one of these wars. Would *I* go? For my father, there was no question. I think the fact that his father served in World War II might have something to do with it. A faith in country. A sense of loyalty that I've never experienced. But my father wanted to get his degree before he enlisted, so he found himself at the local draft office to request an extension. He described the scene: "Amazing, all of these guys trying to get out of the draft. Guys were crying, wearing dresses, and bringing in their girlfriends. I had to stand in line with all of these hippies with their mothers and their ministers. When I finally went before the board, eight serious men and women sat at a long table, and I sat down in front of them. The first thing they said was, 'Why are you resisting?' And I told them, 'I'm not resisting! I just want another six weeks to graduate college.'"

The draft board told my father to get out of their office, that processing his appeal would take months. Bureaucracy was on his side. Six weeks later, he graduated with an associate's degree in business and he took a job at Sears, just like his father did in 1946. For a few months, my father lived in a cheap apartment on the edge of Grand Rapids, Michigan, until he got his draft letter. Forty years later, he still remembers the exact date: March 12, 1971.

My First Memories from a 15-inch Zenith. My first memories are drenched in yellow and orange. This is one of the side effects of being born in 1977, a time when images possessed a slightly nauseating hue. What was going on with film processing during the late 1970s and 1980s? The photographs and films of the forties, fifties, and sixties were defined by stark contrast and luscious Technicolor and then, somewhere in the seventies, images began to look overheated. Was it Pan-O-Vision or Color by Deluxe? Who do I blame for a childhood that is sealed behind a tacky yellow-orange resin? More importantly, where can I go to complain that many of my first memories were cobbled together by fragments of television shows, that much of my early knowledge of the world comes from scripts in Burbank, California?

Here is my first memory: I sit in a high chair in front of a small TV. I am alone and the opening credits for a sitcom play something like *Happy Days* or *Laverne & Shirley* (programs that were centered on their own peculiar nostalgia for the 1950s). A shenanigan involving a character kissing a mannequin plays out on the tiny, oversaturated screen and it scares the hell out of the two-year-old me. I scream.

My parents will tell you that I was too young to remember this. They might be right, for I no longer have much faith in which of my memories are manufactured and which are real; however, their brows furrow when I describe the shag sepia carpet, the cracked yellow vinyl of the high chair, and other details that I should not remember. I think they're embarrassed to admit that they parked me in front of a TV.

So I'm screaming while Potsy or Squiggy or some oily sidekick mugs at a dismembered mannequin, and my father rushes into the room, pats my head, and calls me "big guy" before switching the channel and then the memory fades.

Here's another story: I am lying across my parents' bed watching afternoon TV while the reassuring weather of my mother steaming and folding shirts fills the house. This is where my friend Mr. Rogers spoke to me, this is when he sidled up to the television every afternoon and told me that I was special, that I was the sole reason for his endless routine of sweater changing and puppet handling. I truly believed that Mr. Rogers existed for me alone and, in retrospect, he worked hard to cultivate this falsehood. He knew what he was doing.

One day my cousin came over and told me that he wanted to watch Mr. Rogers. My world fell apart. I screamed "Liar!" and I attacked. My parents had to pull me off cousin Nicky, whom I was punching and clawing like only a four-year-old gone feral can do. This is how I learned that everybody watched TV.

Detroit Mythology. Just beyond the stadium, everything goes dark. Keep following Jefferson Avenue south, veer off to the left, and it's a world of charcoal sky and industrial scrap, punctuated only by the dotted lights on the cables of the Ambassador Bridge. Canada lies quiet in the shadows a quarter mile to the east. Strange ash is everywhere. The first techno shows were held here in the 1980s: legendary three-day parties held in abandoned warehouses and auto plants, fueled by little more than a drum machine.

I grew up ten miles to the north, but it might as well have been a hundred. My parents rarely went downtown in the 1980s. I remember the *ker-chunk* of the doors locking whenever we crossed Eight Mile Road. "It's safer," my dad said. And of course I began to conjure bloody scenarios of masked robbers ripping open the doors of our Pontiac and dragging us onto the pavement. This was my introduction to the city. In high school, I snuck into Detroit every chance I got. Sometimes I went to parties in factories. More often, I simply drove around aimlessly and looked at things. The city was forbidden and fascinating. And what does it say about us, that we let such magnificent buildings fall into ruin? They are an indictment.

Dead buildings hulk together in odd clumps, all husks and dust — the collapsed lung of a once healthy and rational organism. Everything is empty, hacked out in gray. Fully grown trees live in some of these buildings, their branches punching through the shattered windows. A tangle of cinder block and rebar surrounds the footprint of the abandoned train station, designed by the same architects who built New York City's Grand Central Station. This old building serves as a bottomless well for Detroit's urban legends: battle royales where bets are placed as crackheads fight to the death, disemboweled German shepherds on candlelit altars, snuff films with drug-addled cheerleaders from the suburbs.

Even without the stories, this place can be hard on the nerves. You have to admire the guts these kids had, hauling synthesizers, turntables, and generators out to places like this. Boards and rusted chains crisscross the doors, weather-stained notices and permits from the city are jammed into cracked plastic sleeves. The gargoyles and wainscoting were stolen long ago, along with everything else that a desperate mind might deem valuable.

I was there only twice and sometimes I wonder if it existed at all.

Afternoon Drive Through Babylon. I drive down Woodward Avenue on a Sunday afternoon, moving slowly along the main artery that runs into the heart of Detroit. The cafés and boutiques of Ferndale jump-cut to the crinkled and scorched buildings of Highland Park, which fade into the uneasy arrangement of Detroit city proper. The scene beyond my windshield becomes unbearable: beautiful broken buildings with trees poking through dusty glass on overgrown lots; concrete deserts and bricked-up mountains, barbed wire and rusted chain link — the accumulated evidence of a chilling indifference that has been designed into the city's way of life.

Detroit. The word conjures metallic dystopia and gritted teeth steeling for a blow, the sight of abandoned buildings coated with defiant graphics, and the sound of an echoing kick drum and a synthesizer growl. This is the muscular arm of the American underground — think of the music and design this city has given our nation — but it's also the bastard kicked under the table and living on a gritty floor after a hangover of red-lining and blockbusting, a whispered threat to industrial cities everywhere, a notch in the belt of corporate profit margins , and a punch line (see the standby t-shirt with the image of a gun that says, "Welcome to Detroit, Sorry We Missed You"). Detroit is America's bogeyman. Hyperbole is easy when it comes to discussing Detroit.

People wander in the middle of the street, some drinking, others glaring. The next block features an enormous and well-preserved Catholic church with a trim electric green lawn. Next I see people slumped in the median and a few blankets pitched like tents along the curb and then comes the Detroit Institute of Arts. This is followed by a row of empty storefronts from some 1950s vision of a shopping heaven that went south a long time ago. Then out of nowhere, a brand-new stadium that sends suburbanites in khaki shorts and tucked-in jerseys scuttling through the streets as they seek the safety of parking structures. Poverty, wealth, and civic institutions play a wicked game of cat and mouse for ten long miles until Woodward finally deposits you at the river's edge, confused and rattled at the foot of the Joe Louis memorial. It's fitting that the avenue ends with a sculpture of a giant fist.

This sort of schizophrenia is to be found in every American city. We accept poverty as a plain fact, a fundamental rule of the game, forgetting that there is a living, breathing mayor of this scene and a government that has done nothing to fix this city. No state of emergency has been declared. We continue to vote for this sort of negligence and people like me will drive through it, telling ourselves that this is somehow just a fact of modern life. Nothing to be done about it. Unless it suddenly shows up uninvited on CNN after a hurricane — then we get indignant and pull out our checkbooks. Poverty happens all the time, it's just ratcheted up several notches in Detroit, where we've been promised a renaissance for decades (even the city's key architectural feature is named after the idea).

I did not appreciate the psychic impact of growing up on the edge of a wounded city until I moved to New York. The appearance of working streetlights does not make the front page here. There are no jubilant editorials when a new store opens. When I made a remark to my students about Devil's Night, I received confused looks. I was surprised to learn that most Americans attach no significance to October 30 and it was only when I said out loud that "Devil's Night was a day when people set abandoned houses on fire" that I understood the incredible things we are capable of taking for granted.

Hitchhikers. There's camaraderie on the interstate. We pause to look at accidents. We slow down to watch people stranded by the side of the road. Sometimes they're hugging themselves, staring at a fresh wreck. Or they're bent over their popped hoods, frowning at their engines. Sometimes they're scary, holding their shoes and grinning at the traffic and you wonder how they got out here in the first place.

Somewhere in Virginia, a clean-cut kid stands on the edge of I-95 holding a cardboard sign that says "South" in serious block letters. Everybody's whizzing past at ninety miles per hour and it's getting dark. What's he going to do? In South Carolina, a young couple walk along the shoulder of the highway. The girl waves a sign and the guy has a guitar across his back. Her sign also says "South" but it's written in cursive and has a festive border. They seem like they walked out of an old movie and for a moment I envy them.

A few miles north of Daytona Beach, an old man waves and grins on the entrance ramp. He's covered in mud and has the durable look of somebody who's spent many years in the sun and the wind. Even though he's holding his thumb in the air desperately, I keep driving.

I do not stop for any of these people. Would you pick me up if I were standing on the side of the road? I drive alone because there's no more room. Having somebody else in the car means worrying about what's on the radio, monitoring my speed, and apologizing for a passenger seat covered in books, empty Nicorette wrappers, gas station receipts, and dirty clothes. But I wonder what it'd be like to suddenly have a stranger in your car, particularly one who thought that writing *South* on a piece of cardboard was their best way to get someplace.

I-95. A girl in a dirty tracksuit sits bunched up with a sign against her knees: *Pregnant + Homeless = Please Help*. It's Christmas Eve. A wild sun sets behind the new casinos, throwing gold light everywhere. I continue walking down the boardwalk. Against a shuttered t-shirt and novelty kiosk, a half-man sits, no, he's *placed* next to a beaten hat with a few quarters. His torso sits on a wood plank with wheels and he blows into his fingerless gloves. I keep moving, lost in dumb thoughts about losing a few pounds and how I'd bungled everything the last time I seduced somebody and how cold it is out here. Then the images of the pregnant girl and the crippled man hit me hard in the gut and I turn back. I want to give these people all of my money but they are gone. I try to imagine where they went but I can't even guess.

Two days later, I'm gazing at the faded headshots of missing children at a rest stop just outside of Jacksonville. Most of them are runaway girls, their faces digitally altered to show how they might look today, five or ten years after they disappeared. Big hair and no baby fat.

I point the car west and head to Little Rock, feeling old and apocalyptic and convinced that I will get run off the interstate by one of these wicked semi-trucks with a logo for Walmart or In-Sink-Erator.

Home. My first memories were made in a ranch house in a suburb with a reassuring name like Fairfield or Warrenville. I ran through sprinklers and listened to the blue zap of the bug lights at night. I helped my mom with her little tomato garden and chased after my dad with a plastic lawn mower while he cut the grass. Our grass. The house was brand new and I remember driving with my parents to watch the construction before we moved in, my dad pointing as the foundation and frames and siding added up with each weekend visit. I didn't understand their excitement at the time, but I knew these trips made my parents very happy. I grew up with a driveway and a patio and a plastic wading pool that got cracked and filled with leaves by autumn. We were happy. Then we moved away. Later, I believed we were happy because we owned a house.

Motel. One night at a cheap motel in the Mojave desert, I dozed to the hum of the soda machine and the occasional shifting of the ice box. When I was small, I lived in a series of motels with my parents when we arrived in Detroit. I thought it was a grand adventure at the time and I loved the sudden rupture to my routine.

There was a kitchenette but we ate fast food and my parents halfheartedly told me that we were on vacation. I kept this fantasy alive for a while, but the dead leaves in the empty swimming pool and the charred lawn next to the I-75 service drive soon forced me to accept that this was not a holiday; this was our life. If it were vacation, my mother would not have been crying so much. My father still would have chain-smoked, but not in such a tight-faced and mechanical way.

We moved to Detroit because my father was looking for work. It wasn't going well. When I picked up on this I went to pieces. I had no friends, and even if I were not tragically awkward I stood zero chance of making new ones. The motel held no children within its cinder-block walls, only old ladies waiting out their pensions, leathery alcoholics, and young men who slept all day. I invented a brother and named him Max. My parents quickly bought me a Cabbage Patch doll and told me that his name was Max too. Looking back, I realize that they simply didn't want me jabbering at thin air.

Twenty-five years later, I can think of few things more melancholic than a sun-bleached Coke machine glowing in a concrete stairwell — and yet it's something I am deeply drawn toward.

Sprinters & Bounders. Daytona Beach. Say it out loud. The cadence is great, so classy and clean. *Daytona Beach.* I knew nothing about it except the name, but after staring at my road atlas along the side of Route 98 in Alabama, it became the climax of my drive through the South: a good place to see the ocean and have a reflective moment before pointing the rental car back north.

I hit Daytona Beach late on a Tuesday night in hurricane rain. The empty flooded streets are draped in blinking neon and checkered flags. That's when it finally clicks: the Daytona 500. Spring break. Why didn't I know this? Here is a city dedicated to driving on the beach, which is one of the most American activities I can imagine doing. I grab a pizza and a motel room on the edge of Atlantic Avenue where the rainwater is ankle deep. Forty-two dollars for a single room with a mirrored wall, the NASCAR Fan Special.

The next morning I went to the dog track and watched the greyhounds run. Then I poked around the parking lot of the International Speedway, a monstrous stadium draped in logos and swimsuit models holding cans of beer. If you drive around the back to Airport Road, there's a gravel path that leads to a mini-society of recreational vehicles: hundreds of Coachmen, Weekenders, Sprinters, Nomads, and Bounders huddled together in anticipation of the Pepsi 400 NASCAR Nextel Race, which is four days away. White lines are spray-painted across the grass, defining the boundaries of this itinerant community with its own trash bins, newspaper boxes, and trailer churches. The *Daytona News Journal.* Central Florida Raceway Ministries.

Families sit in folding chairs drinking beer in foam holders, poking at small barbecue grills. Sunburnt men stand solemnly in small groups with their hands on the hips of blue jeans and tracksuits, narrowing their eyes and critiquing one another's trailers. Flags fly everywhere: American and NASCAR and Confederate and Miller Lite and Jesus Saves. I drive up and down the grass, marveling at the size and complexity of this thing. NASCAR is one of the most popular sports in America, second only to football, and in terms of product sales its fans are considered the most "brand loyal." This isn't just brand loyalty; this is a culture. But what does it mean to drive your family thousands of miles to watch other guys drive in a circle? I want to ask somebody but a mean-looking guy in a pickup truck with a security logo cuts me off and jerks his thumb toward the exit.

Fourth of July. In Florida, an angry crowd surrounds a wholesale fireworks store on International Speedway Boulevard. Two security guards beat them back but the families yell and shove, refusing to form a line. Fireworks are a big deal in America, generating close to one billion dollars in annual revenue. Cross any state line and you'll find dozens of stores selling you whatever the law allows.

Firecrackers, skyrockets, roman candles, bombs, and sparklers are all forbidden in New York. Cherry bombs, tubular salutes, repeating bombs, aerial bombs, and torpedoes are banned in Mississippi, although you can purchase other fireworks if you're at least twelve years old. Items that propel themselves through the air are banned in Florida, but snakes, smoke devices, and trick noisemakers may be sold anytime. "Items that explode by friction are banned in Nevada." (I'm sure there's a good joke in there.) In Nebraska, colored sparklers are prohibited but gold and silver sparklers are permitted. Chalk one up for states' rights.

As night falls, I stop in Waycross, Georgia, where dozens of families sit in folding chairs in the parking lots of Burger King, Walmart, Walgreens, and Sears, waiting for the fireworks to begin. In the darker corners of the strip mall, kids sit in the beds of pickup trucks, teenagers hold each other, and big shirtless men lift their babies in the air. Everybody faces north where the fireworks bloom and pop from the high school football field behind the Walmart. The grand finale fades and there's chaos as a tangle of headlights, horns, and engines dart down the side streets and scatter into the darkness.

AM Radio Scan. "— yeah, I used to be a Boy Scout and these days I take kids to the Boundary Waters area in northern Minnesota and up into the mountains there and, well, I lost my camera and I'm wondering what kind of digital —"

Turn the dial as I drive past a sign for a combination air conditioner repair shop and peacock farm. A straw man is stuffed into a radiator on a pole. After a week in the Mojave, this sort of thing seems normal.

"— we've seen everything disappear! If you have debt, you can't adjust quick enough for the times that are coming. We're going into the worst depression in our country's history. It's not about building wealth anymore, it's about survival."

Turn the dial and anxious callers argue about shadow governments, remote viewing, and invisible runways in the desert called "cheshire strips."

Army, Part II. "After I got my draft letter, the army rounded everybody up in Chicago," says my father. "Man, what a mixed group! We took a bus down to Fort Polk, Louisiana. It was my first time down South and I remember passing KKK billboards along the way. Basic training was eight weeks of hell for some guys, but I was in decent shape. Marching, running, exercising, and learning to shoot a rifle was just another day for me." My dad sounds tough as he says this. He tells me that he volunteered to clean the latrine because it gave him an extra half hour to sleep while he waited for everybody to get out of the showers.

I can't imagine going through basic training. I go to pieces if I need to wake up before nine o'clock. Sometimes I crave the ruthless discipline of the military. I think about what I was doing when I was twenty-one: skipping class, brooding, switching my major from Japanese Literature in Translation to Playwriting to Graphic Design and getting stoned while working the zombie shift at a gas station or rolling up carpets at an oriental rug store. It would have been nice if somebody kicked my ass out of bed at six in the morning and made me do some push-ups.

After basic training, my father landed a comfortable gig as a clerk typist in Fort Rucker, Alabama, where he filed hospital intake records until he was shipped to Vietnam in January. He took a plane to Seattle, where he awaited his assignment. I try to picture myself sitting on that plane, knowing that I was heading into a bloody war on the other side of the world where, in many cases, there was a 30 percent chance I wouldn't come home. I picture him sitting on that plane, trying not to think about the rumors or run the numbers: the life expectancey of a machine gunner is eight seconds, etc.

"I still don't know what happened in Seattle," says my dad.

"Most guys spent a few hours in the holding barracks before they were shipped out. I spent several *days* sitting on my you-know-what until my orders were changed to Korea. No idea why. Maybe they had enough clerks in Vietnam, who knows. It was fine by me. I knew some of the guys who were coming home dead and I had no plans to be a hero. I wanted to get home as fast as possible."

My father comes alive as he tells me about his flight to Korea; it was his first taste of the world. "We refueled in Alaska, where I got to smell the negative-fifty-degree air. A quick stop in Japan, then onward to Seoul, where I sat in another holding area until I was assigned to the Eighth Army, which is the same army that Grandpa was in. Same shoulder patch on the uniform."

He was offered a job in the DMZ as the head typist, a voluntary position with extra combat pay and "pleasure girls" brought into the camp. He laughs. "Yeah, I pissed the colonel off bad when I refused. Your grandpa told me to never volunteer for anything in the military, and I listened. A few months later, I met the guy who took that job and he told me it was a living hell with Communist propaganda broadcasting over PA systems night and day."

He was ultimately assigned to the bomb squad. He kept regular hours and was given his own jeep, so it was a pretty cherry job. He drove around Korea, deactivating old landmines from the war. "I did that until November, when I got called home by the Red Cross on emergency leave. My mom was very sick. I lived in Chicago and commuted every day to Fort Sheraton."

Soon after, my father was released from the army. He remembers that day too: March 11, 1973. "I was finally a civilian again, and I went back to Sears in Grand Rapids, where I met your mom and a couple years later along came you. Well, I guess you know the rest."

Stroke. In the summer of 2006, my grandfather stepped out of a movie theater and thought it was 1956.

Fathers. A thick old nurse gets on the hospital elevator and takes a split-second glance at the two tattoed kids with pants hanging around the knees and gargantuan white t-shirts before asking, "So who's the daddy?"

"I am, ma'am."

The other kid says, "Mine was born a few months ago. I remember you."

The nurse nods. "Of course you do. And if I track you down in eighteen years, will you still be there?"

Both of the kids laugh. "Sure. Right." They exit on the maternity ward and when the doors close the nurse shakes her head and slaps the wall. "God damn it. I mean god *damn* these kids. You know?"

I can't think of a thing to say. Driving home, I see a billboard that says, "Have you spent time with your child today?"

The Hoist Points Will Hold, Part 1. I watch the curbside arrivals and departures: passionate kisses, cold pecks on the cheek, old ladies holding hands, men clapping each other on the back or sometimes just throwing a sharp nod. I duck into an airport bar owned by the FOX Sports Network because it's the only place that still allows smoking. Dozens of screens line the walls, all tuned to FOX News. California is on fire again. Beheadings and explosions. The banks have no money. Senators debate whether they should debate the war.

I crush my cigarette and head to my gate. Watching CNN headlines while scrolling along the E-Z Walk makes me feel important. There's a developing story on the giant flat screens: a threatening note was found at the Lincoln Memorial. *Do you know what anthrax is? Do you know what a bomb is?* The anchorwoman looks radiant as she tells us we'll be taken live to a press conference in just a few minutes.

I'm jittery. When I get back to New York, I'm going to drink tea and protein shakes. I'll get big arms and I'll have an easygoing attitude. I'll know what an antioxidant is. I'll eat whole wheat, not white. I will quit smoking when I land. I am not prepared.

My grandfather is sick and alone up in Michigan. My grandmother died a few months ago, and now he lies in the hospital recovering from a stroke. He looked washed out and angry when I saw him. There was no dignity in the recovery wing of the hospital; there weren't any of the things that I associate with my grandfather. Not in a facility with dusty rose walls and Christmas decorations made by the long-term residents.

I love the airport. Everything else drops away. I can think at the airport. It's the anonymity of time and place: Tuesday morning and I could be going to Denver, Amsterdam, Beijing, or Mexico City. You don't know. On the screens, Hazmat teams descend upon a bottle of Gatorade found in the men's restroom. A bomb squad corners a suspicious coffee cup in a stairwell behind the memorial. The world is falling apart because my grandfather is ill.

At the hospital, I cornered a nurse in a pink hallway and peppered her with questions. I wanted to see the paperwork, I needed to hear promises. Poking around the old cottage in Michigan, I found a box of photographs in the basement. Square photographs with scalloped edges. Men in fedoras with cigarettes and defiant faces standing in front of airplanes, Studebakers, sailboats, and fighter planes. People and places that I do not know. I need my grandfather's explanations, his memories.

I sit near the windows and watch the airplanes, reading the text on the fuselages: *Keep Away. Lock-out Position.* A small torn label says *The Hoist Points Will Hold.* I repeat this to myself like a mantra. This just in: it was only Gatorade. It was just a cup of coffee. A murmur of disappointment rises as the crowd breaks up from the giant flat screens and everybody returns to their assigned gates. We line up for the boarding call: a loud family in matching t-shirts, a salt-and-pepper executive in a perfect suit, an old man in a wheelchair, a beautiful girl with a guitar, a fat man in shorts. I watch the TVs, waiting for the next security briefing.

Flags, Past and Present. My grandfather is giving away his possessions. I sit next to him on the small sofa in his tidy little room at the old folks' home. A beat-up shoe box sits between us, filled with tie clips, loose change, yellow letters, pocket watches, and birth certificates. I pick up a tiny dog-eared and time-stained book. I crack the cover: *Cleanse the lepers and cast out demons.*

"That's the Bible my parents gave me when I went off to France," he says. "I carried it with me the whole way. You want it?"

"Sure. Did you ever read it?"

"Not really. But there's some good stuff in there."

He gives me a gold coin that he received after a long night spent hauling lumber for a neighbor. We ping-pong across the decades. He tells me about the time his aunt hopped a fence in Detroit and marched straight into an army barracks, demanding to be a nurse. "That's one of the few stories about Queenie that I'm sure is true," he says. Before I can press for more details, a photograph stuck to the side of the box grabs his attention. "Now here's a picture of me and my buddies with our boat. Man, we used to sail!"

I ask why he has so many Mexican coins and Japanese bills. "Eh, who knows how these things happen?" He tells me that pennies were made out of zinc during the war because they were using copper for ammo. "Now here's a picture of my mother cutting my hair so I could save money. And this looks like an old shell cartridge . . ."

I pull out a crinkled photograph of my grandfather in uniform, a young man with a neatly folded flag tucked under his arm. At the bottom of the shoe box I find an old yellow clipping from a local newspaper in Flint, Michigan. I show it to him with a dramatic flourish, expecting a flash of pride and perhaps a few colorful stories about his brush with fame. Instead, he looks it over and stabs at the part that says *His Favorite Food*. "I never liked chocolate pie! Especially not with whipped cream. Darn it, they just made that up out of the blue."

flint folks
by Thurston S. Jenkins

SGT. JAMES A. REEVES
908 EAST SECOND STREET
U.S. ARMY ~ 8th AIR FORCE

CHIEF-OPERATOR in charge of a RADAR CREW

BORN IN FLINT (AT 908 E. 2ND) HE GRADUATED FROM CENTRAL IN 1941 AND ATTENDED JUNIOR COLLEGE FOR 1½ YEARS B.A. (BEFORE ARMY)

JIM ENLISTED IN THE ARMY RESERVE CORPS NOV. 20, 1942 AND WAS CALLED TO ACTIVE DUTY IN MARCH, 1943. HE RECEIVED HIS INITIAL TRAINING IN RADAR AT DREW FIELD, TAMPA, FLA AND HIS OPERATIONAL TRAINING IN MISSISSIPPI AND ALABAMA

FOR THE RECORD

ARRIVED IN ENGLAND IN JAN. '44 AND TRAINNED AGAIN—WITH ENGLISH RADAR EQUIPMENT. IN AUG. '44 THEY WENT TO CHERBOURG, FRANCE, ON HARBOR DEFENSE—THEN TO PARIS— AND FROM THERE TO THE FRONT LINES IN BELGIUM—THEN BACK TO LE HAVRE ON HARBOR DEFENSE AND FROM THERE TO WIESBADEN GERMANY WHERE THEY "FINISHED THE WAR" AND WHERE JIM WAS TRANSFERRED FROM THE 9th TO THE 8th AIRFORCE FOR DUTY IN THE PACIFIC —HIS 4 BATTLE STARS ARE FOR NORMANDY, NORTHERN FRANCE, CENTRAL EUROPE AND THE RHINELAND.

THE BIGGEST EVENT IN JIM'S LIFE WAS HIS MARRIAGE, ON SEPT. 15th, TO MISS VIVIAN SHORT.

HIS FAVORITE SPORT- SAIL-BOATING

HIS FAVORITE FOOD

CHOCOLATE PIE WITH WHIPPED CREAM!

POST WAR PLANS- JIM—AND "MRS. JIM"—ARE GOING TO FINISH COLLEGE—TOGETHER.

Me at War. Late at night, when I'm surrounded by old photographs and heavy nostalgia for a time in which I have not lived, I sometimes wish I went into the military like my dad and my grandfather and his dad. I know that anybody who saw action in a war would tell me that's a stupid thing to wish for. But it gives you an idea of how mixed up I am.

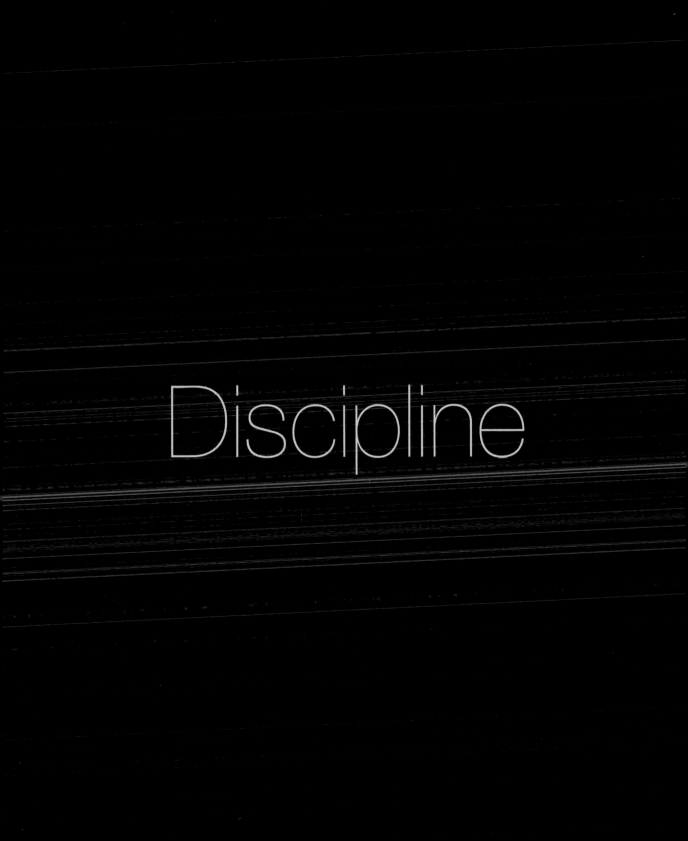
Discipline

What does it mean to be a man? A man does not raise his voice. A man can quit cold turkey. A man can be alone with his thoughts. For me, something must always be on. I need screens. Right now the TV is saying "the outfit should have its own point of view, the dress should have an outlook." Maybe it's time to get rid of the TV. Not just turn it off, but bury it in the closet or better yet throw it in the East River.

Lying on the bed next to a stack of books, I try to read Amis, Vollmann, Mailer. An attempt at self-improvement, but nothing sticks. It's a few minutes past midnight and I'm still wearing the day's shirt and tie. I don't want to relax. It occurs to me that I will never be a professional boxer. I'm getting old.

I sneak glances through the window across the alley where two big beautiful girls are getting dressed to go out. Watching the pilot light on the heater glow and fade. Waiting for a catastrophe, a reason to unplug and to run, to get basic and brutal in some far-flung mosquito-soaked village.

What do I do? I make images. I fuss with typefaces, color palettes, and pixels. I live behind screens, conducting my life in 72 dots per inch. I should be a soldier. Hardcore military, making tactical decisions down there in the muck, crawling on a cut six-pack with a dripping blade between my teeth. Racing across hard-packed tundra in the middle of the night while searchlights sweep the horizon.

You must become tough. Strong like nails.

These words play through my head, wrapped in a stern Russian accent. Why is my mind manufacturing imaginary Russian advice? I do not know where these words come from. Probably a snippet from some action movie circa 1985, back when Russians were the stock villains. Regardless, the phrase offers sound advice because I am not tough, certainly not like nails. To achieve any degree of toughness, one must have a goal. A reason to be tough. My goals in life remain well hidden.

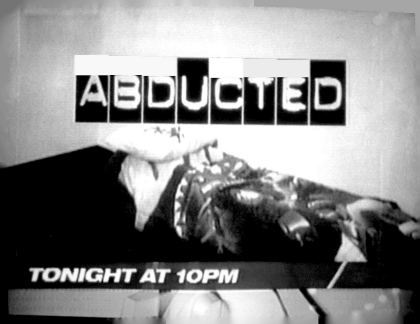

It is impossible to concentrate. There's all that noise from magazines, TV, e-mail, Google, RSS feeds, billboards, cellphones, and cameras. The media will not let me rest. And I shouldn't. Something could happen at any moment. The average American sees 3,000 advertisements every day. Nobody gets through this unscathed. There is a reason that words like *viral, target,* and *campaign* are the vocabulary of marketing. They used to show newsreels in movie theaters; now they show commercials. My psyche is a battlefield and I cannot disengage. I often fall asleep to the 24-hour news cycle, comforted by the simple knowledge of being plugged into something that will keep going with or without me.

Every morning I pay for the sins of overexposure. Endless chatter and fragmented images lurk beneath each day's arrival into consciousness: bits of bad movie dialogue, news headlines that my sleepy mind has scrambled and reprocessed into gibberish. Advertising jingles, the evaporating scraps from last night's dreams, garbled headlines and e-mail subjects that make no sense, to-do lists insistently forming, murmuring voices reciting the imaginary results of online polls, those sparkle-eyed CNN anchors with flipped hairdos and exotic cheekbones — now sex gets mixed up with terror alert levels and all the rest of it. The news watch never stops. Every morning I stand at the sink wiping away the sleep and my mind is so fuzzed over that it is difficult to locate my own voice, my own internal monologue. I once nearly brushed my teeth with my razor. You have to pay attention.

Climbing stairs is an effort. I am out of shape and I want to sit down. But the elevator is on the fritz and I'm running late. Sweat drips and my legs explode. This is nothing. I think about the Olympics. Little girls were crying and the cameras hounded them mercilessly, intent on transmitting every last sob and shudder.

Picture it: a twelve-year-old girl crumpled on the ground, her life destroyed because she could not stick a landing. It was terrific TV. And it was the first time I took an interest in the Olympics. I'd like to believe this was the result of a newfound interest in athletics, a desire to witness the outer limits of the human form, but I really wanted to see if anything was going to blow up, to find out if the terrorists were going to fill in the blanks left by the media and their endless quizzing of security coordinators and bomb experts.

Adults were also falling down at the Olympics, crashing into hurdles and falling on their faces. I became addicted to watching perfect bodies do impossible things. Sitting on the couch or tucked into bed, munching Cheez Doodles and drinking Coke, I looked at the cords and planes of muscle on display and thought about my body. Aside from a few confused appearances at the gym just after the new year, my promises to live like a Spartan athlete go unfulfilled. In the mirror I can see the beginnings of a gut perilously balanced on my hip bones, ready to leap any day now; my arms are shapeless afterthoughts, Play-Doh cylinders, and in the right (or wrong) light my chest is convex. This is my prime.

War & Peace. An elderly man and woman trade memories of war. Their words rise and fall in the café, sometimes landing near my table. *Who never came back. Who was never the same. Dirty business.* The man's voice hardens as he explains how you kept yourself clean in the trenches with only your helmet, your finger, and your bayonet: "You'd fill the helmet with water. First you start with your teeth, then you shave, and only after that would you move on to the wounds — you start with the cleanest parts first and the dirtiest last. A lot of guys didn't bother to do that and they got terrible infections. We lost a lot of men not from bullets but from shaving badly."

There is a lesson here and I try to pay attention, but a well-dressed woman walks by and now I'm thinking about how high heels on concrete sound like a beautiful metronome and that I should finally learn to tie a double Windsor knot. I'm also distracted because I cannot remember what Tom Brokaw looks like. I can picture all of the major news anchors except for Tom Brokaw and it's driving me nuts. There is no discipline in my head.

And check out this phenomenally old Chinese guy: you can catch him in Chinatown at seven in the morning, standing in the middle of Mott Street. Dressed in flip-flops, football socks, striped blue and pink shorts, and a natty black Batman t-shirt with a missing sleeve, he's firmly planted there on the pavement, hands clasped behind his back, puffing a cigarette and pointed north, gazing up at the Empire State Building, not giving a fuck — not about how he looks, not about how others look, not about the traffic, not about anything. Every morning I rush past him on the way to the office, jealous as hell.

Crime Notes. I saw a girl get caught stealing the other day. She darted through the store, weaving expertly through racks of clothes as a giant security guard gave chase. As she reached the exit, another guard stepped in front of her and she crashed hard into him, spun around, and attacked the first guard. You could hear her little fists beating on his chest. A mannequin teetered, then fell over. Everyone in the store tried not to watch, tried to keep up the pretense of shopping, fidgeting with the merchandise while the guard pinned the shrieking girl to an expensive chair with a swoopy back. She flailed and beat at his chest. "You tried to bite me!" he shouted.

Now everybody was staring. She continued to struggle and deny everything, even when they pulled the stolen merchandise from her bag: a purple sweater and a pair of gloves. You could hear her crying over the high-energy dance music. It was an embarrassing and ugly thing to watch but it would have been exciting if it were on TV.

Last week on Sixth Avenue, a frantic man darted past me, pushing people out of his way. Another man followed in hot pursuit and collared the guy a block later, knocking him to the concrete and kicking and punching like hell. One man was rolled into a sniffling ball, the other was raging: he kept hitting and stomping, stopping only to kick a newspaper stand before spinning around and spitting on the guy.

"Welcome to New York, motherfucker!" He said this like it was the movies. There was a thick crowd and nobody said a word except one girl who muttered, "Just leave him alone, man." Some people shook their heads. Others cheered. Nobody did anything and I just walked by slowly, thinking about how I'd probably write this down at some point.

Gas & Liquor. In some parts of the country, gas stations function as community centers: people come in for newspapers, lottery tickets, nachos, gossip, hunting supplies, flavored coffee, and beer. Sometimes they have showers and meeting rooms. In Nevada, they have slot machines. In Pennsylvania, I stayed at a motel inside of a gas station. Some sell liquor, some don't. Either way, kids hang out in the parking lot at night.

You can tell a lot about a state by the way it handles its liquor. In Utah, only beer with low alcohol content is sold in stores. Waitresses are prohibited from offering a wine list unless the customer asks for one, and food must be ordered. In Tennessee, wine is sold only in liquor stores, and these stores can sell *only* alcohol. No corkscrews, no daiquiri mix, not even a bottle of water. In Nevada, alcohol can be sold almost anywhere 24 hours a day and public intoxication is perfectly legal (in fact, there's a state law preventing any town or county from making it an offense). Minors in Wisconsin can drink, as long as an adult is present. Absinthe is legal in Missouri.

Mini-Mart. A girl with spooky dark eyeshadow and big bleached hair slams two bottles of orange Gatorade Xtreme on the counter next to the two pints of Tropica watermelon liquor that the cashier has waiting for her.

"Doing it again tonight, huh?"

"That's right," says the girl. "You got to try it sometime. This shit is super easy to drink and you get so fucked up. Hell, I don't even know how I made it home last night."

"Honey, you need to take it easy."

"Tonight's going to be even better. The guy I'm going with now, he's got a bottle of tequila. It's going to be crazy, right? But after this, I'm done."

"You'll be back."

"I know."

Somewhere in Texas at two in the morning. I drive along a string of oil fires that light up the yellow dirt road, and I think about how I would make a terrific trucker. I love driving ten or twelve hours at a stretch. The simplicity of getting from A to B without crashing into anything is tremendously gratifying. Feels like I'm getting things done. The rest of the time, I'm sitting in front of a screen or talking about abstract concepts that are beginning to lose their usefulness to me. Back in New York, I'm teaching a course about the history of American education while running a small design firm, but out here in the middle of the desert night, that feels like fictional work. My life ought to be as physical and workmanlike as driving.

Dawn breaks and the landscape begins to change. Shattered barns. Epic clouds. My highbeams flash on clumps of bushes and sandy ditches. There are no more trees. I am in the West. The stars are sugar white and giant insects compete with the radio. I drift into strange memories of fidgeting during childhood assemblies in the gymnasium or moments when I behaved badly to my parents or how I was too shy to talk to anybody at school and I'd come home and count the words I'd said that day. Or that awful period when I smoked weed all the time, wore ridiculous clothes, and thought I was a poet. I bought swag from two drag queens on the edge of town and I thought I was edgy. I was a bad alcoholic writer who never wrote anything.

Now I'm falling asleep at the wheel but it doesn't matter because there's nothing to crash into out here.

Florida. Flipping through the radio, a man sings: "You say I'm weak, I think you're wrong . . ." Idling at another traffic light, I watch a woman with an elaborate hairdo fix and fuss until it looks just right. The Space Coast is dismal: a beautiful ribbon of sand covered in big cinder-block stores along the ocean's edge. Jiffy Lube stands next to the World's Largest Selection of Adult Videos with flecks of the Atlantic in between.

Florida gives me violent vibrations. At night I dream of guns: pine crates of automatic rifles and surface-to-air weapons packed in brittle hay. Gigantic helicopters dropping boxes of guns into the most frightening parts of the world. Blades beat in the middle of the night and searchlights sweep across jungle canopies and desert floors while thousands of starved and frightened people scramble for boxes of pistols. I probably saw this on TV.

In Key West I watch the sunset with hundreds of pink and tipsy couples. As the sky goes red, the men pull their wives closer, stand a little straighter. What kinds of promises are they whispering to themselves?

AM Radio Scan. Somewhere outside of Reno, a preacher shouts. "Temptation has no respect for anybody! Temptation don't like children, he don't like old people, he don't like men, he don't like women, he don't like blacks, he don't like whites, he don't like yellow people, and he don't like green people, if we have any of them on the face of this good earth. The devil, the archenemy of God and man, hates *you*. Period."

Hard cut into Hank Williams doing "I Saw the Light" back in '48 and dead drunk by 25 — *worries and fears I claimed for my own, then like the blind man that God gave back his sight, praise the Lord, I saw the light. No more darkness, no more night —*

Punch the button and some guy's screeching about how there are no Bibles in places like North Korea and that's why things are so terrible over there. "And where there used to be Bibles in hotels in America, there's now on-demand pornography. We have a debased, corrupt, degenerate society! We don't understand what freedom is. We think pornography is freedom. We think using drugs at all times of the day, *that's* freedom."

Somewhere Over Pennsylvania. The twin engines drone and a baby babbles beneath the reassuring hiss of manufactured air. The scrape and rustle of pages: *The Wall Street Journal*, spy thrillers, the Sky Mall catalog (lighted indoor palm tree, $259.99). Somebody reads an article called "George Clooney on the Burden of Being Sexy."

I try to read Graham Greene but none of the words gel. It's not his fault. I want a cigarette. The plane could fall out of the sky and I'll have given up smoking for nothing. Staring up the corporate gray aisle, I pretend it's 1962: everything is mint green and sedated blue, the air is filled with smoke as torpedo-chested stewardesses hand out Lucky Strikes and highballs to square-jawed businessmen who make heavy use of the metal ashtrays in the armrests while cracking jokes and inventing nicknames. A drowsy mambo issues from the tinny speakers, blending with the laughter and joy of an airplane filled with carefree smokers.

Graham Greene is closed. I munch nicotine gum and stare at other people's headlines and personal media players. *A New Obstacle to Peace. Managing Your Hedge Fund. The Healing Power of Antioxidants.* Everybody has the latest gadget and it looks so much nicer than the one I bought two months ago.

The Hoist Points Will Hold, Part 2. I'm taxiing out of Detroit Metro again. My father had a stroke last week. He came home from work as usual and, as he told my mom about his day, his words degraded into jibberish and he fell over. Baby talk. He spent two weeks in the hospital, babbling and drawing pictures. I'll never shake the image of my dad sitting on the edge of his hospital bed, confused and frustrated and unable to form any words.

My father followed his father's lead: he was drafted into the army and took a job with a big company. By the time he started working for Sears in 1973, there was no more working your way from the stock room to the conference room. Transfers, then layoffs. Manufacturing plants closed and one of his bosses went to jail. My father's job in the textile division was scratched out and he drifted from job to job, only to find himself being replaced by kids with MBAs. He smiled through all of this, waiting for something to work out because, after all, he played by the rules: he served his country, he started a family, he landed a job at a big company. He still followed the old codes, believing in firm handshakes and follow-up phone calls. A shirt and tie under burgundy sweater, itchy slacks, and neatly parted hair. Next came the pyramid schemes and a brief stint at a butcher counter. Now he's in speech therapy, a stroke victim just like his dad. Except he's only 56 years old.

Ready for takeoff. I stare at the engine. I read the labels on the wing: *Pivoting Door, Lock-out Pin, Start Valve Handle Access, Keep Away Lock-out Position 414 AR 414 CR. Hoist Point.* Watching Detroit's grid shrink, I sort out the parts I like from the ones that scare me. I make promises: work long hours and hit the gym. Get disciplined, tough, and jacked. Read. Love her well. Write (doesn't matter, just write). Save your money. Travel. Remember: whole grain, not white. Jump into the middle of things. Talk to people.

I drift into fitful airplane sleep, dreaming movie scenes: the man putting on his army uniform and polishing the brass before kicking out the chair; a couple running toward each other in the pouring rain. I wake up and look for information in the grids of corn and looping cul-de-sacs, in county roads and city blocks.

The doctors said my father might not work again. He might not drive again. He might not even be able to speak. But he recovered. One day he drove to the store. A few weeks later, he found a job managing the lawn & garden department of a big box store.

God

What does it mean to be a man? A man feels centered and calm. A man can stretch out and relax on the beach. I squirm in the sand and stare at the horizon. Rich retirees splash around in the sea, playing with a yellow raft. They're all very happy and brown and wearing Speedos and shouting *bueno*. Next to me, my lady friend sleeps peacefully while I fidget in the white hot sand, squinting at the cottages on the hillside, staring at my fingertips, shutting my eyes and watching the dots. I feel morbid and I don't know how to stop it. It strikes me that I don't know anything about death or even pain. I've never lost anybody close to me or lost a lot of blood and although I'm grateful I feel unprepared.

The Home. Listening to the screech and static of AM radio, I speed through the center of Michigan, racing past shattered barns, rusted filling stations, bait shops, and strip malls. Old big band tunes drift across voices howling about the second amendment and anxious callers connecting conspiratorial dots: fire and brimstone, traffic accidents, terrorist strikes, and factory explosions. Last night a man tried to chop off his arm in Monterey, California. He thought he injected an air bubble after shooting up, so he grabbed a butcher knife and . . . I change the station and hear a man say, "You got any advice on the best place to buy a thousand rounds?"

I'm relieved when I pull up to the retirement home and see my grandfather standing there, waving and preparing to say golly gee and look how tall I am. We talk. He says he wants his wife back, that he wants to live in his house on the lake with her again. "But I've been lucky," he says. "I've had things my way for a long time. Now it's time to do things their way." I don't know who *they* might be, but it sounds right and I try to look brave, saying that everything will be okay.

My grandfather stands in the parking lot with his cane, waving at me as I drive away. World War II and a family and a career and he disappears in my rearview mirror. I turn on the radio and people holler about oil and family values. They yell about how this country is no longer what it once was. I leave my grandfather back there, at a nursing home bookended by a McDonald's and a Walmart.

God. My mom was raised as a strict Catholic. Nuns hit her in school and she was excommunicated from the church for marrying my father. He was a Methodist, which basically meant potluck dinners in a chapel with Astroturf and a preacher who played the guitar.

When did I first understand what *God* meant? I dig through my earliest memories, back when everything is a fog and there are only a few coherent scenes to choose from. These few glimpses are vivid yet unchained from any timeline, given shape by the old Polaroids that provide my only sense of who I was for my first four or five years. When it comes to understanding God, I have two key memories.

1. Crouched on a yellow linoleum floor, I feverishly rubbed a white crayon onto a dark blue piece of construction paper with all my might. I still remember feeling a little crazy while doing it. I titled the resulting white blur "God," writing this in the bottom right corner. The strongest part of this memory is feeling quite certain that I had uncovered what God looked like and not understanding why my parents weren't more impressed with it.

2. Rolling around on a thick orangey carpet while my parents sit quietly on the couch. All of us are watching the pulsing globs of light that function as angels in *It's a Wonderful Life*. Even today it's an unnerving sequence for me, far too existential for a Capra film.

These are my first impressions of God and I'm not sure which came first, the construction paper or the movie.

Belief. Sometimes I hear church bells ringing and I'm surprised by how much they comfort me. A call for ritual, a desire for order. I envy the devout. I admire religion as an attempt to seek some kind of moral pattern in a scary world — but I refuse to accept it. My rejection is nearly physical. I have trouble understanding people who believe in magic, chakras, and ghosts. But *why* am I so antagonistic toward anything spiritual? My interior life probably pales in comparison to a monk's. I would like to pray or meditate but I cannot sit still. Yet if it feels better to believe in something bigger than ourselves, why not? Why not take comfort in the idea that one day we might see the ones we've lost? Because I worry that faith is a form of denial. Because I believe that it's a stubborn refusal to turn on the lights. I do not think this is a good quality of mine.

Where Will You Spend Eternity? There's not much to do along Route 207 in northern Florida. People speed across it on their way from the Atlantic to the Gulf. In front of a Kangaroo gas station, several families wave handwritten signs that praise Jesus, ask about our sins, and warn of eternal hellfire. It takes a moment before I register the image of a little girl holding a sign asking, "Where Will You Spend Eternity?" I turn around.

Leaning against the rental car, I watch the families wave their signs and chant. They're really fired up, but nobody slows down to listen. A man whizzing by in a pickup truck gives them the finger.

I walk over. "Convert anybody yet?"

One of the men grins and offers his hand. A firm and slightly frantic handshake. "No, of course not! We don't convert people. That's not why I'm out here today. I'm here simply to spread the word of the Lord. Jesus spoke to me and that's why I'm here."

"Does the church pay you to do this?"

"Absolutely not!" He says he's been out here for about three hours and that it's a blessing to be here, serving Jesus. "I was very lost a few years ago," he says, "but then I found the Bible. Like you, I was skeptical, but did you know that everything in the Bible is scientifically proven?"

He tells me about his church, about how it's saved the life of everybody that I see here on the corner today. He tells me that people often yell terrible things at him from their cars. Can I take his photograph? "Of course!" And he calls the wife and kids over and they pose with their signs. I thank him and wish him luck and he goes back to chanting at the traffic with his family.

"Take His Hand, Not His Life." The interstate is a violent place: the brutal architecture and aggressive billboards, the zoom and the noise, the roadkill and shredded tires. The exit names are chilling: Dead Man's Pass. Starvation Hill. Poverty Flat Road. Cement Plant Road. Power Plant Street. The deer-crossing signs are riddled with bullet holes.

Religious signs. *Jesus is watching you. Be sure of this: you are dreadfully like other people.* Signs to keep your baby and stay off the meth. *Smile! Your mother chose Life! Abortion is murder!* A gigantic billboard flashes and nearly sends me off the road: *You Are My God (flash) And I Shall Earnestly Seek You. Death Is the End of Excuses. Death Is the Beginning of Eternity.* The bottom of the sign says "Highway Evangelism" and there is a phone number to call. I dial and a nice man tells me about spiritual life and relief efforts in Haiti.

A fresh wreck up ahead: the trailer hangs off the edge of the overpass, its back broken, and there is no vehicle attached to the hitch. People look over the edge, some with blankets around their shoulders, others with their hands clamped over their mouths.

Runner-up. Somewhere at the bottom of Texas, a woman on the radio says, "I was born to be Miss America. In my heart I knew that the pageant needed me and I knew that my country needed me. I'm not saying this to be arrogant, it was just a plain fact, you know? And I won pageant after pageant until finally I was up there on the national stage and that's when the unthinkable happened. And as my hopes flashed before my eyes, I realized that God had a new plan for me, that Jesus had come into my life, that I belonged right here, telling people like you the good news . . ."

Religion in America. A woman on the Brooklyn-bound F train told everybody that they were going to hell during rush hour. She wore elaborate leather boots, a gray wool skirt with a matching jacket, and a maroon scarf. She was not asking for money. She had a proper hairstyle and nice earrings. She was not insane.

"Should you get hit by a car today, that will not be the hand of God, it will be the work of the Devil!" She blurted this out and launched into a lecture about religion — the fire and brimstone kind of religion built on salvation, temptation, eternity, sinners, devils, repentance, the Lord Jesus Christ, damnation, and the antichrist. She said these words and many like them in a steady voice that was just a few clicks below shouting, yet loud enough to disturb my reading. I wasn't particularly interested in the *New Yorker*'s ten-page essay about neuroeconomics and ballerinas, but I resented being unable to continue. I tried to imagine what her God must look like, pumped up with teeth bared and throwing lightning bolts from a crashing cloud in an apocalyptic sky. I looked up and saw only advertisements for drinking diet beer, curing erectile dysfunction, and getting a job parking cars in Manhattan. The subway is no place to think about your soul.

At the Second Avenue stop, an old lady in a floppy purple hat pushed past the preaching woman. She flashed a bright smile and said, "I wish you good day, Ma'am, but you're full of shit." The preacher waved a hand at the closing door. "Sister, I wish you a good day, too," she said, "but unless you accept the Lord Jesus Christ into your heart, I fear that your days shall be" — and back to the hellfire.

An old man who looked like a giraffe sighed loudly and shook his head. Some people rolled their eyes and snorted, others loudly refolded their newspapers and snapped the pages of their magazines. They would not be deterred. "And in their freedom, they will fall into the abyss of the Devil," she said.

I tried to make progress with neuroeconomics, but the words were drowned by talk of redemption. I stared at the shapes on the page, pretending to read them, even turning the page to convince others of my fortitude. "Harm only those people who do not have the seal of God on their foreheads," she cried.

Enough. I dropped my magazine and stared at the woman. She had a nice purse and fuzzy gloves. Like I said, she was neither destitute nor psychotic. If she were crazy, I wouldn't have asked her to quiet down. Public ranting is the one privilege we grant the mentally ill. Everybody else must go through proper channels.

"Excuse me," I said. "You've made your point. Can you please move to another car now?" My voice came out thin and watery. It was the first time I'd caused a scene on the subway.

"You move!" she fired back in a voice that was clearly experienced with causing scenes. "I can see that you do not repent your sorcery or your immorality or your thefts!"

"My sorcery?" People were staring at me now and I had no choice except to press on. "You're the one disturbing people, so why should I move? If your faith tells you to love and respect your neighbor . . . "

She leaned over me and smiled. "And I do love you, brother, I really do. That's why I am here this evening, warning you —"

"Lady, I agree with him," said a thick man with a pink face and a crew cut. "Why don't ya take a hike? We've heard enough." He made a sharp gesture with his thumb. "Move it along."

A teenager leaned over and whispered something to his girlfriend and they erupted in nasty laughter. Soon all kinds of people were telling her to be quiet and shut up and fuck off and get the hell out of here.

She stood there and took it. Eyes closed with a martyr's grin, her face was zen and I admired her for it. She tugged at the ends of her scarf and launched into a new sermon about how she could brave the ridicule of the damned because even the smallest number of believers was strong enough to suffer the abuse of the masses. A tiny middle-aged woman with enormous glasses cried out that there was "no way in hell that Christians were oppressed in America." More shouting erupted. Sometimes four or five voices were arguing with the preacher and with each other. I returned to staring at my magazine, feeling like I just broke something.

We reached the Jay St.–Borough Hall stop and the woman got off the train, still reciting her verses about hell and salvation. The old man who looked like a giraffe tucked his newspaper under his arm and looked hard at me. "You gave her exactly what she wanted. You know that, don't you? Best thing to do is just ignore them. Let them keep talking."

Yes, but I could not concentrate on my reading.

Overheard in Times Square. "They just keep going on and on about that evolution shit and it needs to stop already," said the cop. "Next thing you know, scientists will have us believing we came from spiders. I don't know about you, but I ain't no monkey without a tail."

Neon Cowboy. Along the dead straight line where Utah meets Nevada at the edge of the Salt Flats there's a town called Wendover. Established in 1906 as a stop on the Western Pacific Railroad, Wendover is divided by the state line. The Utah half is Mormon country, where tobacco and cigarettes are sold under the counter. The Nevada state line starts at the wall of a casino.

You can stand right in the middle of Route 93, one foot in a land of 24-hour booze, gambling, steak, and hookers and plant your other foot in a Mormon county where caffeine is verboten — and right there, that's America's brainpan. Protestant versus profane. America's work ethic split into two. God versus devil. Go into the desert and invent your own religion. Or build a monument to 2-to-1 slots, live nude girls, and an All You Can Eat Sirloin Buffet.

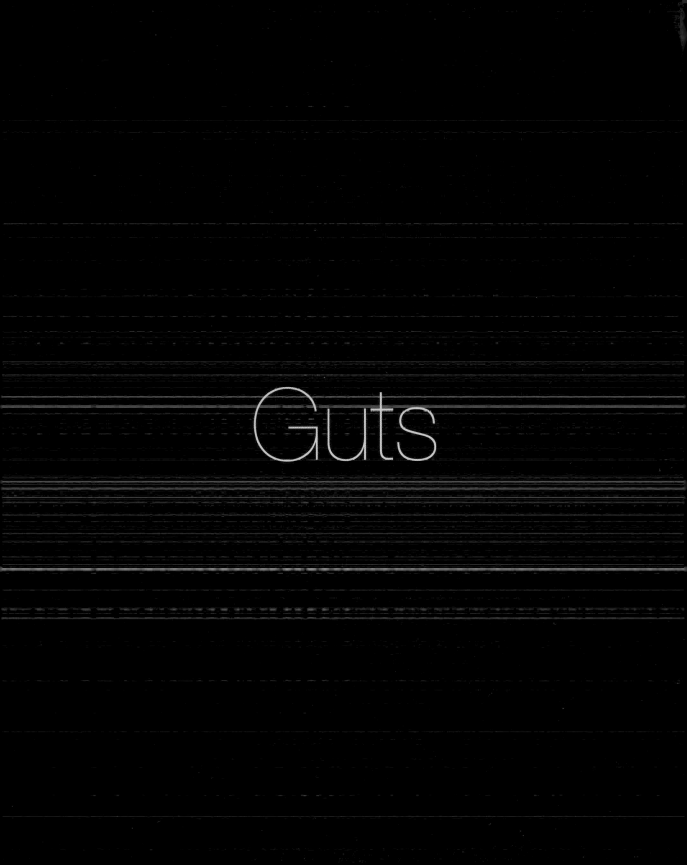
Guts

I have never been in a fight.

A woman has never thrown anything at me.

I worry that something is lacking in my life.

What does it mean to be a man? A man gets up at dawn without complaint. Maybe he can lift his own body weight. Perhaps he's got a bit of heft. Regardless, he has presence. He knows how to move. He's taken a few punches and knows it's not so bad. He can handle himself. I see these men, the way they move through a crowd. Strange how you can pick them out, the confident versus the anxious.

Look at my great-great-grandfather. He built a cabin with his hands. He got up early. He fed people. Every generation sings the praises of the ones that came before. Our ancestors were always tougher, braver, and more honest than we are today. They did what needed to be done. I can't picture anybody saying that about me.

September 11. Six, seven, eight, nine years later and still nobody knows how to mark the date. First off, let's never use the word "anniversary." We'll keep working, but we'll mourn. And I work late tonight. When I leave the office, twin beams of light play against the clouds and fog, going spectral blue and gray. I walk two blocks to where it happened. There are souvenir stands with paperweights and coffee mugs, and temporary walls with architectural renderings, optimistic signage, and the names of the dead. I stand there, fighting through the rhetoric and sloganeering, looking past the grainy videos of bearded men taunting us, trying to see around this confusing war and the lapel pins and all of the we-shall-never-forget and fight-them-over-there. And it's so damned hard to shut out the noise and simply see these names for what they are. For who they were. Flashes keep popping, everybody's documenting everything. Uploading. Posting. Commenting. People pose for pictures, grinning and flashing peace signs. FDNY and NYPD stand clustered together beyond the chain-link fence, visibly upset.

A very old man with a thick white beard sits against the wall of names playing "Amazing Grace" on a thin steel flute and people kneel down to take his picture with their telephones while some guy chatters behind me about paperwork that needs to be filed ASAP and somebody else whines about not having had sex for two days and a group of girls giggle at a text message and I look past the rows and rows and rows of names and see the American flag draped across the side of the American Express building and I want to scream.

Witching Hour. It's a few minutes past midnight in Washington, DC, and Pennsylvania Avenue is empty except for a drunk guy stumbling in front of the White House yelling, "Are you a good witch or a bad witch?" Three cops suddenly appear and carry him off.

Protest. Tired of complaining. I want to make a difference. I want to stop the killing and support the troops and make everything okay. One morning I grabbed a car and drove to Washington, DC, to protest a war. The news networks had already covered the protest before it happened: *thousands gathered across the country on Saturday to express their dissatisfaction with the war and, although upset, there were no unexpected incidents.* These days, protests are an expected part of the news cycle. There is no shock or surprise; they've been defanged.

A mixed bag of people got together on the Mall: NYC District Council 37, black power groups, women for peace, people concerned about mortgage rates, Filipino liberators, pot legalizers, DC Civil Service Technical Guild Local 375, Justice for Katrina survivors, Queer Empowerment through Solidarity & Truth, Pittsburgh School Bus Company No. 151, the Lutheran Peace Fellowship, people who want health care coverage, Iraq Veterans Against the War, Free Palestine supporters, immigrant rights activists, people against a possible war on Iran, and various vegans and vegetarians.

The chants were straightforward: The people united / Will never be defeated. Hey hey ho ho / The troops have got to go. They say more war / we say no war. Ain't no power like the power of peace 'cuz the power of peace don't stop. What do we want? Peace! When do we want it? Now! 1234 / We don't want your racist war / 5678 / We will not cooperate!

People carried signs that said things like "Ignorance is a weapon of mass destruction." Stop the killing. Democracy . . . some assembly required! Stop the war. Fight racism. No first strike on Iran! Wage peace. They won't hear us until they fear us. Holy wars suck. More love. Our president eats the flesh of murdered animals. Learn why we should all be vegan! Anybody find those WMDs? Dissent is patriotic. Impeach, convict, then execute. Health care not warfare. Peace is a family value. A vegan diet is the only peaceful diet. Legalize marijuana now. Iranians are good people. Don't kill them. Breasts not bombs (carried by two large topless women). Impeachment: so easy, even a Congress can do it. Queers against war and patriotism. Fuck war.

And a tiny old lady with flowers in her hair held a handwritten sign that said, "War is not good for children and living things."

Non-Incident at Penn Station. An enormous old woman with no teeth sits in the waiting area surrounded by everything she owns. Camouflaged men with guns patrol the station with alarmingly perfect posture, mechanically scanning the crush of tourists and commuters while talking from the sides of their mouths. Two soldiers stop and watch the old woman.

I lean against the wall with my suitcase at my feet, watching the departure boards click and change. Perplexed by a job I no longer understand, I need to get out of the city and look at some new scenery. Babylon, Deer Park, Ronkonkoma. No phones, no screens. Looking at the strange names on the board, I realize that I know nothing about New York beyond Manhattan and Brooklyn. Maybe I should just go home and get some work done.

I look back at the old woman, jealous of her serene gaze. Framed by a patchwork of dirty cardboard, plastic bags, and stained blankets, her red face grins as she knits a scarf from a bright red ball of yarn. Maybe it's a sweater. In the corner, a TV screen talks about an anthrax scare in Washington, DC, but she pays it no mind. One of the soldiers walks over and makes a show of checking his watch. "Three-hour limit, ma'am. You've been here for four. Time to move on."

She gives him a giant smile and says okay but does not move. He crosses his arms and waits. "Now, ma'am." She beams. Her fingers never drop a stitch. "I am. I will. In a minute. I'm not bothering anybody, son."

Unsure what to do next, he adjusts his cap and fingers the strap of his shouldered M-16 rifle. Her eyes dart to his gun and her smile fades. I head to the ticket machine and buy a ticket for Greenport, the end of the line. When I return to the waiting area a few minutes later, the old woman and the soldier are gone and the 24-hour breaking news channel continues playing to a bank of empty seats.

Saturday Night Fish Fry. Memphis is a mean city on the edges. Grizzled industrial buildings and coils of barbed wire smash up against neighborhoods where people sit on busted porches and glare at the traffic. Old men in dark suits stand in the road, sipping beer from paper bags. I'm lost, looking for the Stax Records Museum, and when I get there it's closed. I eat fried fish while screen doors slam and somebody on the radio sings about *being a catfish, baby, a bottom-feeder deep in the sea, and you better think twice before you try and catch me.* An old TV flickers, showing a commercial for motor oil with adaptive molecules. I head to the Mississippi River, where the low-slung paint-peeled homes give way to newly renovated lofts and a sleepy Arts District.

I walk up Beale Street, a blaring neon pedestrian mall that lives somewhere in a back alley behind Times Square and Bourbon Street. The main attraction is walking around with enormous plastic cups of beer, and a municipal sign for tourists apologizes: "Today, old Beale Street lives amid the rebuilt environment mostly as a memory for people who experienced it and as a symbol for those who've only heard its name." In the past, the street was a swinging jumble of millionaires, prostitutes, magicians, and proto rock and blues. It was, says the sign, "a few blocks of brick and cement where the well-heeled and down-and-out could hope and dream and have a life." Where is that place today?

Sitting at a sidewalk bar, I talk to people. When I tell strangers that I'm from New York, they usually want to talk about September 11. Was I there? Am I scared it will happen again? Those bastards still need to pay, they say. I do not want to talk about September 11 and I usually mumble something vague, hoping to change the subject. "Let the tigers come with their claws," I say. I picked this up from *The Little Prince* and I have no idea what it means, but it sounds heavy and usually stops the questions.

I do not want to talk about September 11, but a boozy woman in a bright pink pantsuit keeps going: "Memphis'll be a target, just you watch. We got some major attractions here and in a year or two they're gonna attack us. You just wait and see." There is no fear in her voice, only a screwy pride as she keeps pushing this point. She wants me to agree that, yes, her city will be terrorized. And I understand this: we want to be at the center of things. Everybody wants to be world class.

People taking pictures of people taking pictures. New York is such a well-documented city. People point cameras at every street corner, at the tops of buildings, at each other. Fifty people and a buffet table surround the filming of a *Law & Order* triple-homicide investigation outside a Chinese grocery. A few art students are staging something on the steps of the subway stop at Bowery. A kid in a pink fedora says, "Just go ahead and shoot me in the wheelchair, then push me down the stairs." A hard-angled model seduces a green Buick on Crosby Street. She wears a poncho, rope belt, and a pound of green eyeshadow. She's splayed across the hood and somebody says "brilliant."

Cameras click and beep on the corner of Broadway and Houston: people crowd around a plastic subway car, snapping photos with their telephones and clever digital cameras and high-grade equipment attached to umbrellas and directional microphones. They take pictures of the guys spray-painting the plastic model of a subway car. They take pictures of each other.

Twenty-five years ago, graffiti was a dark art: illegal and political, it was the omen of a city falling apart, and it was the opening salvo of an invisible city inventing something brand-new despite playing against a deck stacked with red-lining, blockbusting, and a negligent government. Kids climbed over razor wire to get into the yards and they ran from the police. Some were locked up; a few died on the third rail. Today, the media are invited at noon and it takes place beneath the vacant gaze of an enormous girl in her underpants.

Truck Stop. In Wyoming, I speed past a gorgeous old semi cab with a vintage paint job and I hit the brakes and slide into a dusty lot filled with sleeping bulldozers and columns of razor wire. I snap a few photographs, disappointed that I can't capture the majesty of this shimmering machine in the middle of all this desert. A gigantic black SUV with tinted windows crunches into the lot, spraying gravel and covering me in dust. The window lowers and a big old man with a brush cut, black suit, and black sunglasses nods at me.

"Afternoon."

"Afternoon."

"What are we doing here?" he asks.

"Just taking a picture of that great truck."

He looks over at the busted truck, then stares hard at me. "Damn it to fuck," he mutters. "Get the hell out of here." The tinted window slides up and he spins the SUV around and watches me.

Truth Seeker. I'm slapping enormous New Mexican bugs against my neck and talking into a bulletproof window.

"Nonsmoking if you have it."

"We don't."

I give the lady in the purple robe thirty dollars and she shoves a key under the glass. She has curlers in her hair and she's ticked because I woke her up at two in the morning. Still, I need to know: "Why is this town called Truth or Consequences?"

"You remember that game show in the fifties?"

"Not really."

"Well, we really liked it."

She flips off the light and goes back to bed, leaving me in the dark.

I later learned that the name was adopted in 1950 when the radio quiz show *Truth or Consequences* announced that it would broadcast the program from the first town to rename itself after the show. A town in New Mexico called Hot Springs followed these instructions.

12 Hours in TJ. In San Diego a woman named Aloha Taylor does the weather on the radio. I drive through the night. Crossing into Mexico is too easy. There are no traffic stops or checkpoints and I don't realize that I'm on the other side of the border until I hit the traffic and push-carts and red signs to *alto*, which everybody ignores.

It's cold in Tijuana tonight and I'm the only magnet for the pushy hawkers on the broad sidewalks of the Avenue Revolución. The inn-keeper takes me aside and tells me to be discreet when taking out my wallet. She worries about my safety, but the city seems fine: trinkets and exotic dancers, plus a surprising number of monster-size discount pharmacies, bright fluorescent coolers with bottles of Viagra and Avian Bird Flu repellent and white-jacketed clerks dozing behind the stainless steel counters. There is a gambling hall filled with strange combo bingo/slot machines that nobody knows how to play. I keep mashing buttons and lose a bunch of pesos and decide not to do the math.

The next morning I want to get out of Tijuana and see more of Mexico. I head east on Highway 2. Six minutes later, a motorcycle cop rides slow alongside my window, staring at me. I play it cool. He pulls me over.

"*No hable espanol?*" he says. "Oh, this isn't good."

It is not good. He studies the lease for my Budget rental car and says he's taking me to see a judge, who will impound the car for fifteen days and I will pay a fine and walk back across the border.

"Is there anything we can do to avoid this?"

"Fold the bills and put them in my hand, then follow me."

Ten minutes later I'm locked into a tight grid of cars, inching toward the U.S. border. Back on solid American highway, I drive fast, heading towards Calexico, where I pull over and look through a chain-link fence at Mexicali.

Borderline. Given the hysteria about the Mexican border, it's startling to discover that it's just a modest wood and wire fence. On one side you can see the cluttered housing projects, flapping laundry, and garish billboards that signify the poor; on the other side you are in America, where the towns are also poor, but we have thick coils of razor wire, floodlights sweeping the desert floor, and highly trained dogs barking in the middle of the night.

I head east on the Patriot Freeway, speeding past Fort Bliss and billboards advertising six different factory outlets for cowboy boots. Signs for Vietnamese food, gun shows, and ammo shops. A night with Edward James Olmos. I coast through a deserted Rio Bravo cranking Junior Walker's "Shotgun." Flashlights sweep across trunks and underneath cars. The Department of Homeland Security pulls me over four times to search my trunk for Mexicans. K-9 dogs and security mirrors on poles. I check into a mint green motor lodge circa 1962 that overlooks six lanes of interstate traffic separating El Paso from Juarez. Sounds like the ocean. Searchlights scan the desert. Next door, the border patrol officers drag a TV into the parking lot to watch the Raiders game.

Build a fence and tell the guys on the other side, Good luck with that. People keeping other people out. I'm beginning to believe there are inherent moral problems with a nation that lines its border with guns, dogs, searchlights, and razor wire. I head south on 83 through Zapata to the bottom of America, where I find an all-night laundromat with a guy in a wheelchair selling drugs in the parking lot. It's a one-stop shop for some folks. In the morning, the radio says that 21 people were killed in Juarez last night.

Mojave Holiday. Driving into the desert and going off the grid, searching for the photo magic of airplane graveyards and auto wrecks, all those cast-off machines perfectly preserved in the rust-proof sun. I want to see the edges of those white boxes on the map. Seems like nearly a third of the Mojave requires top-level clearance. Some of it doesn't show up on satellites. Yet this is where America seems to be heading, as brilliant green lawns and the skeletons of monster homes spread across the red rocks.

A town called Mojave on the edge of the desert: trains run along the highway and behind the motel there is an airport filled with research facilities, training academies, and the bones of old planes. I drink gas station coffee over ice and thumb through my atlas, wondering what I'm looking for in these photographs of junkyards and hangars. What is this attraction to scrap metal, wrecked machines, and dead factories? The apocalyptic glamour is obvious, but there is also something dignified about the persistence of these machines.

The names of the hidden places stick in the mind, demanding details: Groom Lake. Chocolate Mountain Gunnery Range. China Lake. And so many strict signs: Lethal Barriers Ahead. No Trespassing. Security Clearance Ahead. Restricted Area. Violators Will Be Prosecuted. Warning — US Air Force Installation. Warriors Supporting Warriors. The liquor store next to the motel has a flashing sign: ice . . . ammo.

Surveillance. A few miles east of the Edwards Air Force Base, a tall girl in a pink bra, yellow short shorts, and long brown legs stands in front of the Texaco station, blowing kisses at the traffic. Six soldiers in desert camo march down the center of Route 58. Farther up the road, a grinning sunburnt and shoeless man with a skinny dog on a rope sits on a plastic red gas container with a box of wine at his feet. In the Mojave desert, you can drive 140 miles without any sign of life, nothing but an endless horizon of baked sand and twisted Joshua trees and then you'll come across an intersection filled with the curious, the wounded, and the mad.

I flip on the radio and somebody says that the lost city of Atlantis was found under the South China Sea. The Mojave is the perfect place to bathe in conspiracy theories. Pieces of jets and tanks litter the floor of the desert. The lights from some of the world's largest military installations glint in the distance and the names out here are epic, front-loaded with intrigue: The Inland Empire. The High Desert. BAE Systems. ASB Avionics. Alpha Dyna Nobel. XCor Aerospace. Derringer. Combat Barber II: Military Haircuts.

In the Mojave, tinted security jeeps appear from nowhere and threaten to take your camera. Or you'll make a wrong turn onto a restricted road and start seeing signs that say things like *Don't Let the Dragon Win* or *Things to do when you return: 1. Put your baby to sleep. 2. Have --- with your wife.*

I crash in a $29 motel in Twentynine Palms. A bar full of marines shoot pool and the jukebox says "I got this truck and a piece of land, a few dollars in a coffee can." I often dream about this part of the country, and somehow I end up here every year, drawn to the combination of the clandestine, the beautiful, and the desolate.

Spaceships land here.

AM Radio Scan. " . . . and that's because *USA Today* did a big story on it and everybody was saying 'Gee, I wonder what it was' and of course by that time they had laid down their cover story, that it was just military flares dropped by the Maryland State Guard and so reporters called them up and they said 'Yes, we flew out there and we dropped some military flares over the Barry Goldwater Gunnery Range at about ten o' clock that night' and so everybody goes 'Oh okay, it was just military flares.' And poor dumb reporters — I don't know what's happening to reporters these days —but they didn't catch the fact that the big . . . *thing* . . . that flew over Phoenix was seen by thousands of people and the videotape happened at eight-thirty that night, not ten o'clock! Yes, there were some lights at ten o'clock, but think how easy that was. Somebody said, 'We've got to have a cover story, so somebody calls up the Maryland State Guard and tells 'em to go out there and drop some flares, which they did.' And later they can say it was military flares, which it was, but that *isn't* what the people in Phoenix saw. Folks, you have to keep up with these stories and you have to think for yourselves!"

"And . . . hang on, Paul . . . and you know that the governor had, at the original news conference back in 1997, I think he had somebody come in with an alien costume and he did his little speech —"

"Yeah, he made a big joke out of it!"

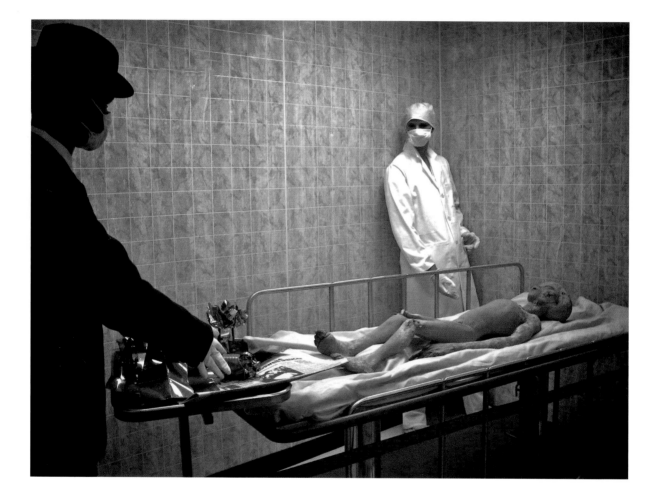

Roswell. A sentence in the promotional literature for Roswell's UFO Museum & Research Center mentions "the government's mass purchase of child-sized coffins" in 1947. Whether you believe in little green men or not, this is terrifying.

The museum's collection includes the radio switchboard that first received notice of a UFO crash, which the army immediately covered up even though nobody alerted the army to the crash in the first place — or something like that. The time line of events is baffling and the official documents are impossible to sift through. And according to the believers, that's exactly how the government wants it to be. On the opposite wall there are dozens of photographs of crop circles from around the world, many of which look like logos for investment firms or pharmaceutical companies.

In Roswell, the McDonald's is shaped like a flying saucer, the Coke machines are decorated with aliens, and the streetlamps look like the big-eyed sketches that turn up in supermarket tabloids. Everywhere you turn, you see the dashed hopes of an aspiring tourist town. No matter how mundane or terrestrial, every business manages to work a little green man into its window display: he's lying on a mattress, riding a bicycle, wielding a power drill, and standing next to a bag of dog food.

Somewhere under the East River. An old man stumbled onto the F train and shouted, "Ladies and gentlemen, can I have your attention?" He wasn't asking for money or selling candy bars. He wanted to rage at us. "Think I'm a loser? Who saved your ass from the Nazis? Who was a cop for twenty-nine years? Me, that's who! Who kept them dopeheads off your streets? Me! Am I a liar? You think I'm crazy? This country ain't gonna suck this man's dick anymore and that's all I'm gonna say to you people."

But it wasn't. He lectured us about Nazis and Russians and Reagan and working the Bronx beat, spinning out a strange toxic mash of American history, most of it shot up with racial conspiracy and secrets that only he understod. Here was a war veteran, a cop, gone fully off the rails. The man across from me sucked his teeth and shook his head. Most people just stared into their newspapers extra hard.

Smile. A stern old man from Finland lectures me on machismo: "Whenever I see a man smiling in public, I assume he's either drunk, mentally ill, or American."

I laugh, and then quickly stop.

"I don't understand why you Americans are always smiling," he says. "You're always telling people to smile. Children smile, not men."

I think about the kids who walk around with a swagger, their faces all twisted up like they're mad at the world. Tough guys wearing their game faces. I used to do that, too. Can't have the world thinking you're a weak sister. But I also remember walking past some guy in Santa Fe who was beaming in a blissed out way — there was no private joke or laughter in his face: he was just happy to be walking down the street with himself. Here's a guy who can fall asleep in a quiet room with his own thoughts, I thought. He doesn't chain-smoke or get upset about trivial things. He never raises his voice. He doesn't always need the company of the TV or the radio or a screen. He can make small talk with strangers. He's calm. And I think that zen smile might be a big part of it.

Making a Friend. The moment I arrive in New Orleans and check into my room, I take a long shower to wash off the Texas dirt and bayou grime. As soon as I step outside I feel dirty again. That's how the heat works here. It's heavy and electric and there's no getting clean.

The rattle and roar of the road still fills my head and I sit on the steps of the Louisiana Supreme Court to get my bearings. A young woman smiles as she walks by. She's cute. She wears linen pants and a fuzzy sweater. She turns around. "You okay? What are you doin' out here at one in the morning?"

"Just got into town. Having a look around."

"Why aren't you on Bourbon Street?"

"That's too loud for me." I tell her that I've been driving across America. She quizzes me about California and New York. She's from Iowa. "I've driven through it," I say.

After a few minutes of chitchat, I nod in the direction of my hotel. "I'm calling it a night."

"Good luck with your trip," she says. "Stay safe!"

An hour later, I'm still too wired to sleep. I go for a walk around the block. After driving through deserts and prairies for a week, it feels good to be back in the arms of a big city, safe under the cover of buildings and listening to the breathing of the traffic and crowds.

I bump into the Iowa girl outside a Walgreens. "You again. Can't sleep, either?"

"We could go back to your room," she says.

"That's a little fast."

"We could have a great time if you have a little money."

"No, I'm — oh. You're not from Iowa, are you?"

She puts her arm around my waist. I imagine what it would feel like, standing in the elevator together, fumbling with the key card. I wonder what position I would request and if I could convince myself that she liked it and how I'd feel when she took my money and the door closed behind her.

Sometimes I wish I was the kind of guy who would do this. You know, reckless and grinning and who cares, if it feels good, do it. But I'm the fool who would pay her for an entire evening just to talk, to find out what it's like to wander around New Orleans on a Sunday night looking for men like me.

Angel's All-Nude Revue. A man and a woman argue on the shoulder of Interstate 10, illuminated by the blinking red hazards of their station wagon. She pounds at his chest and he steps back and belts her across the mouth. By the time this scene registers, they are a half mile back and I'm not sure if I imagined it. I tell myself that I did.

Glum sex along the side of the highway: adult superstores and private viewing booths, a topless and bottomless strip club called Scuttlebutt with giant sun-bleached photographs of women from the early 1980s with enormous mascara and hairsprayed bangs pointed into the night sky.

It's hot in Mississippi, deep in that part of America where it's always dark brick red on the weather map. Swamps and dead black trees, a river dividing east and west traffic on I-10 with neon signs reflecting in the dark water. Sometimes I am driving the only car; everybody else is riding high in SUVs and pickups. What are all of these people picking up?

The radio says that the President and his family might be clones of ancient pharaohs who are preparing for an interstellar war. I think the key word here is "might." The radio is also telling me that pity parties are expensive. Last night it told me to buy dehydrated food because America is on its knees.

The Loneliest Road. The speedometer says 106 miles per hour but who cares? In the middle of Nevada, there's nothing to hit except gold rock and electric blue sky. Out here you can see a car coming from ten miles away. In 1986, *Life* called this stretch of Route 50 the "loneliest road in America." The name stuck.

A spokesman for the American Automobile Association warned all motorists not to drive Route 50 "unless they're confident of their survival skills." You just need a full tank of gas and a lot of time. Route 50 crosses the Great Basin, a blank sheet of land that is larger than Germany. Drive out here and the scale of America begins to make sense. Drive out here long enough and you realize why this is where people go mad in the movies. The names of desert towns seem primed for moments of revelation: Escalante, Delta, Eureka, Searchlight, Orderville. Others are designed for desperation and madness: Hell's Backbone, Confusion Range, Battle Mountain, Badwater, Devil's Hole.

Question: do you slow down because those distant headlights might be a cop, or do you keep zooming along because it probably isn't?

It was a cop. Fortunately I slowed down and he only nailed me for eighty-six in a seventy. He had that thick bleached look of a former high school football star. He grinned at my license. "New York, huh? Is it as crowded as everybody says?"

"Probably."

"I'd go crazy. I'm used to the quiet. Where you headed this morning?"

"Los Angeles. Taking the back roads."

He wanted to hear all about my trip, so we sat together in his patrol car while he ran my license through his computer. I worried that every bad thing I'd ever done would appear on that screen. The computer blipped: *Driver is valid through 2016, requires corrective lenses.* He wrote me a ticket for five over. I've had my license suspended several times due to neglected tickets in Michigan, Kansas, Arizona, and New Mexico, so I immediately turned around and drove fifty miles back to Ely to pay it on the spot.

The Ely courthouse is a classic American building with a cupola on top. Mixed with the thin desert air, it's easy to feel like you're standing in a hermetic backlot for Main Street, USA. A large painting of a sad clown holding a duck hangs in the lobby. I find the cashier's office in the basement and sleigh bells ring when I push open the door, killing the gossip of three middle-aged ladies in bright blouses.

"Can I help you, honey?" asks a redheaded woman covered in jewelry.

I give her my ticket and license.

"You're a long way from home," she says.

"I'm seeing America."

"It's a lot of wide-open space, that's for sure. Great for going fast until, well . . ." She waves the ticket and her bracelets jangle. "Yeah, we know about space. That's all we got out here."

She took my money, shuffled some paperwork, and handed me a receipt. "At least you can say you gambled in Nevada and you lost."

A few voices in the back mumbled. "Welcome to the club."

"Hell, welcome to this town."

Business Plan. The Hotel Nevada is the only casino in Ely with "live gambling" but nobody looks very much alive. Even the slot machines sound tired, giving off rickety clanks and pings for a woman wearing a sweatshirt that says "Drink in Peace." She says "Fuck darn it" like clockwork, providing a steady backbeat for the drowsy country music and the small crowd murmuring at the bar.

Two guys hunch over a table littered with a dead army of Coors Lite bottles. The one with the mustache leans into his buddy and says, "Listen to me, now. All businesses start off in debt. That's just how it goes —"

"But I'm not going to —"

"Let me talk now, Larry. Do you know why all them books say eighty, hell *ninety* percent of small businesses fail? Because they're afraid to take risks, that's why."

"I just don't feel good about —"

"Now damn it, Larry, you ain't listenin' to me right. I'm telling you this is how it's done. You want to get into the drilling business or not?"

Larry stays quiet while Mustache runs through the plan again.

The middle of Nevada gets very dark. I stop at a gas station at three in the morning because it's the only electric thing in sight, a shocking white box on the horizon. Inside the sliding doors, two little kids play on the floor, batting a candy wrapper back and forth. A thin man screams at a video poker machine, telling it to go fuck itself before feeding it more quarters. An impressive ponytail hangs through the back of his red mesh trucker hat, and it swishes wide when he glares at me while I grab a juice from the cooler.

I've interrupted something.

A woman with three different hairstyles at once and mascara in all the wrong places pulls herself up to the counter. Maybe she was sleeping on the floor. "You going to Vegas, honey?" Her breath is eighty proof.

"No, I'm headed to Tonopah and then over to Death Valley."

"Aw come on, sweetie, let's go to Vegas! I know a shortcut and we can be there in two hours."

One of the kids tugs at my pant leg and my first thought is to give her a dollar. I want to make arrests, issue restraining orders, file paperwork with Child Services. I pay for my juice and leave.

Big Fun in Vegas, Part I. There's nobody on Route 93 at one in the morning except for a small man with a brush cut who waves a flashlight across my backseat before giving the go-ahead motion. There's a bit of mountain zigzagging and spotlights and choppers that give you a stadium rush while driving into the neon bowl. Two cigarettes left in the pack, primitive drums and yellow light, dropping out of the red rock onto a grid of flashing lights, hitting the Vegas strip at two in the morning with jangled nerves and no sleep.

The lights at the Mirage freak me out so I move up the Strip to the natty glow of the Sahara, where I sit between a gigantic girl wearing a tight black t-shirt that says "Lick My Taco" and three old Chinese ladies who shout and slap the table no matter what cards they're dealt. The scenery changes an hour later. A little girl sits propped against the sliding doors of the casino, eating fried chicken out of a New Year's Eve party hat. A young couple from Portland fight back tears after losing $35. A trucker from Memphis loses $4,000 in one hand and doesn't blink. I double down with most of my chips on the table, secure in my 20 against the dealer's 4. The dealer takes five cards and hits 21. I smoke unfiltered Lucky Strikes and play for eight hours straight like it's my job. The coffee is strong in Vegas. I get seasoned. I discover that I can nod and wave my hand for hours. I tap the green felt even when I shouldn't, but I win anyway. I'm up $700 and I want to keep going, but I'm getting rattled and everything looks like hell. Stumbling into the daylight, I have no idea what time it is. I gamble the way I smoke and drink and I should probably quit.

Right now somebody is going to pieces here, completely losing his shit, trying to get his story straight before calling home or e-mailing the office or maybe he's crying on the pavement behind one of the skuzzier casinos — *the only $2 ante in town!* — or walking down the strip with a vacant stare, having lost everything and no longer obeying the traffic signals. You can pick these people out from the couples and the families.

There are lots of families here, which is icky because the scene is fueled by sex and money. Business cards for prostitutes carpet the sidewalks and slot machines line the gas stations. Clumps of pawn shops stand at either end of the strip, cracked brick buildings with neon posterboard signs: *Payday Advances! We Buy Wedding Bands! Instant Ca$h for Your Mortgage!*

Flipping another chip onto the felt, I talk to a physical therapist who is moving to Monterey and I listen to a caterer from Virginia describe her new sandwich menu. I try not to count my chips while I quiz the dealer about living in Vegas. "Downtown? Nobody lives downtown," she says. "I'm from back east, you know, and I'd rather live there. But this is the only place where you can save up some decent money."

It depends which side of the table you're on.

Driving north on Route 93 without any sleep, everything's too big and the contrast is too sharp. It's a harsh transition from the dark world of peeking at red and black numbers to something so bright and alien and indifferent. The desert will trash your mind if you're not ready for it. I drive through the Valley of Fire, looking for the Lost City Museum. It's closed. I find a motel with flickering electricity and watch *Law & Order* reruns, which stabilize me until sleep finally takes hold.

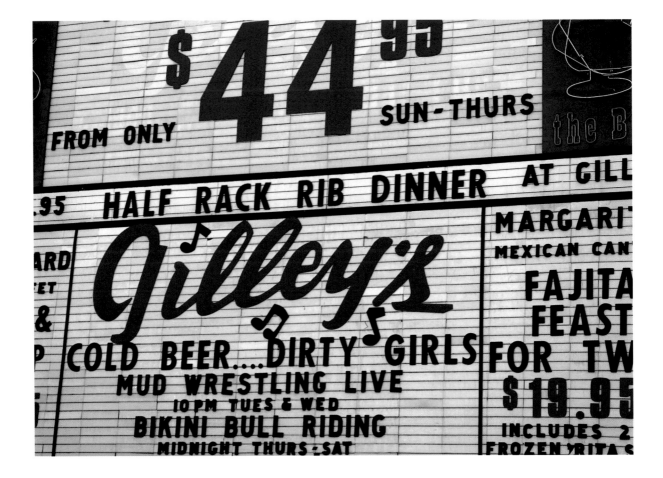

Dirty. I pull over at the scenic overlooks and try to dig the red Utah landscape, but I'm too jittery on caffeine, nicotine, and two hours of sleep. I hit the next motel in a small town called Escalante. A smiley old lady at the desk tells me that she doesn't allow smoking or drinking anywhere on the premises. Or vice of any kind, I imagine.

She quizzes me about how I got to Escalante. "Not sure. I just followed the back roads into Utah," I say. "Just had to get out of Vegas."

Her face gets dark, then brightens: "Well, that's behind you! Tomorrow's another day and if you're heading north, then you're about to embark on the most beautiful drive in America! This is beautiful country, honey."

I hope she's right. It's spooky quiet and I imagine everybody can hear me go to the bathroom. My neighbors sit outside in plastic chairs, an elderly couple thumbing through guide books. The woman says, "If you're parched, they make it awfully difficult out here." She raises a paper cup of wine and puts a finger to her lips.

I walk to the restaurant and a chipper family greets me at the door. "Howdy, thanks for comin' in!" I'm the only customer. After the door closes, they flip the sign to "Closed." It's 7:30. These are the most wholesome people I have ever met. Starched khaki shorts, tucked Polo shirts, bright white socks, and gleaming New Balance sneakers. They glow like a toothpaste commercial, whistling and joshing while Dad takes orders, Mom flips burgers, Junior mops the floor, and Sis puts out tomorrow's pies.

I fantasize about opening my own restaurant. I like the clarity of feeding people. I want to go to church. I want to be a pillar of the community. I reek of cigarette smoke and I've got Vegas neon glazed on my eyeballs.

"Elephant feet," said the old lady selling turquoise jewelry on the other side of the road.

Under the Boardwalk. I hit the Pacific and cut the engine. Standing underneath the Santa Monica pier, I gaze out to sea and wait for one of those feelings you expect when you reach the ocean: the flash of insight that never arrives. I fool with my camera among the heavy wood pylons, taking lousy art school photographs of shadows and water and light. Now here's something: a fight. Fast and messy with hard rabbit punches and pulled hair and then it's gone. People are always more interesting than nature.

Everything Must Go. After two years on the market, the old cottage at the lake was finally sold. A family from Detroit bought it for cheap. That piece of my history is gone now. The place where my great-great-grandfather built a few cabins and launched a perch fishery, where five generations of my family have summered and retired and sailed and swam. There's nobody left in the family to care for it; we're scattered across the country in our own precarious states and none of us can afford to maintain the property. So now it's gone.

Sometimes it's easy to feel like a victim. Sometimes I look through old photographs when everybody looked happy and everything glowed and it's tempting to believe that my family is a victim of circumstance, that we're getting carved up by time, corporations, and bad real estate decisions. But I know that's not true. Things change, keep your chin up, and all the rest of it.

I do not know how to stop this book.

Finland Fight Story. My fiancée was offered an exciting job and I followed her to Helsinki, all the way to the dusty top part of the globe. I thought leaving America would give me some perspective. I imagined myself holed up in a stern library somewhere during the dark winter days, finishing this book while the snow came down and a desk lamp burned late into the night.

Here's how I thought this book would end: after moving to Finland for a year or two, I began to see America in a brighter, clearer light. Although my country continued to frustrate me, I found myself missing the people, the diversity, the chaos, the earnestness. I prepared to return. I started taking care of myself. I stretched in the mornings. I finally quit smoking. Cold turkey. I accepted my addictive personality and made peace with my compulsive tendencies. I bought a pair of sneakers and began running at night. Sometimes I ate salads and seven-grain toast. I got serious. I made commitments: I studied for the law school admissions test, with a vague idea of focusing on something beyond myself. Maybe urban development, criminal justice, or something along the border. On the last page of the book I planned to insert a photograph of me, finishing my first marathon in Helsinki. The end. Fade to black.

And all of these things happened. Then there was a fight.

Oooh, is you talking to your mommy? That's what started the whole thing and it started in a flash, so let me go back a few steps: I run almost every night. After a lifetime of false starts and dithering, I'm finally paying attention to my body. That's what happens after you see your dad sitting on the edge of a hospital bed, talking like a baby.

One night I decided to go for a quick 5k to clear the head. That's the kind of man I'm trying to be: a constructive guy who thinks in kilometers. I lumbered along the Baltic Sea, thinking only of the sweat and the shock on my knees, waiting for the moment when I would slow to a stop, tear off my headphones, clock my time, and enjoy the quiet midnight sunset on my street.

A text message from an unknown number popped up on my phone: *Grandpa Gilewski passed away. Please call your mom.* Except for a few childhood fragments, I never knew my mom's father. I hadn't seen him since I was small. I remember a solid Polish man with a military brush cut and not much else except that he smelled like cigars. My mom was crying when I called. I listened, not knowing what to say. He was 93. He emigrated from Poland when he was small. He served in the Pacific during the war and was one of only a handful of men to survive an attack on his ship. He spent most of his life in the same house in Grand Rapids, Michigan, where he raised five children. I didn't know him very well, but I wish I did. I later learned that he was a brilliant inventor. In the early 1960s, he patented a process for painting seat belt buckles. Powder coating, they called it. He sold it to General Motors and was a millionaire until his accountant fled to Brazil in 1965, taking all of his money.

I was sitting on the steps of a shop on the corner of Uudenmaankatu and Fredrinkinkatu, covered in sweat and listening to my mom cry when two drunk Finnish biker guys came around the corner, slapping each other's backs and roaring. They wore leather jackets and greasy hair and they were pickled in vodka. If they ever owned bikes, they were in the pawn shop now. They stopped in front of me, laughing and chattering in slurry Finnish. I ignored them but they kept shouting.

"Jimmy, who's that? What's that noise?"

"Hang on, Mom."

I stood up and covered the phone. "*Anteksi* — I don't speak Finnish, but please, not now."

"Why? What's so important, huh? I want to talk to you!"

"My grandfather just died and I'm talking to my mom so please —"

Biker Finn #1 started flexing and bumping his chest into me. "Oooh, is you talking to your mommy?" He grabbed at my phone. I caught his wrist and pushed him. I pushed him hard. He staggered back and Biker Finn #2 charged. I'd like to tell you that I was heroic but I wasn't. I was angry and here were two people who deserved a beating. They were thick and sturdy guys, the kind of guys who go out for a fight every weekend, but tonight they were soaked in vodka and easy to push around. I wanted to keep fighting because I felt so helpless compared to what was happening on the other end of that telephone.

If there's a good time to get into a fight with Finnish bikers, it's not when you're on the phone listening to your mother mourn the loss of her father. I put up my hands and backed away slowly. They stood in the middle of the street, confused. Later that night I woke up confused, too, as I replayed the thing in my head. Confused by how quickly a fight can escalate. Confused by how much I enjoyed it.

After my grandfather's funeral, my mom fell down the stairs.

The hospital said her liver was failing.

I ran the Helsinki marathon. I made awful time but I finished it. After the race, I called my dad. He was at the hospital. He said that my mom was very proud and that she was having a good day. He told me not to worry. She was going to be fine. If her ammonia levels continued to stay low, she might even be transferred to a rehabilation center within the week. It was a very good day.

It was my last day in Helsinki.

Faith. I spent hours on the phone, booking and calculating and reciting reference numbers and confirmation codes. I listened to hold music and voice prompts and airport abbreviations. I punched the furniture. I held the line for forty-two minutes, listening to canned jazz with tears in my eyes. I gritted my teeth. For the first time, I thought seriously about God. She would be okay. I was not going to pack a suit.

And so I boarded another plane, this time from Helsinki to London to Chicago. I rented a car. I didn't know how long to book the Honda. A few days, a few weeks. Everybody said not to worry. Everybody said everything would be okay.

I drove to Grand Rapids. I read bad fiction in fast food parking lots. I thought about my mom, teaching me to read. She was so proud that I could read when I was very young. She'd tell everybody about it, and it was mortifying. When I graduated high school, she gave me a copy of Hemingway's short stories. In the cover flap she wrote: *Someday another mother will be inscribing one of your books to her child.* It didn't register at the time, but now it hits me harder every year. That book is my favorite thing. Amazing, to have somebody believe in you like that.

August 23, 2009. Lights flashed. Buzzers buzzed. The PA squawked *code blue*. "Do you want me to code her or not?" There was a horrible argument in the hallway as the doctor explained what a DNR form meant. *Do Not Resuscitate.* I kissed her cold yellow forehead. They took her pulse and called it.

I'm sorry, Mom.

Somehow I got outside. I crumpled on the lawn next to Woodward Avenue. Traffic blurred and I bawled and hollered with the sun in my eyes. Then I wiped my face and collected my father. I filled out forms. A nurse hugged me and said "Oh honey." A doctor clapped my shoulder and said we did the right thing. We drove home.

That night I sat on the porch of my parents' house, listening to crickets and traffic from the interstate. My father's house. A dog barked. A screen door slammed. I could hear my dad shuffling through the halls, sighing and staring at photographs. I told him to pack a bag. We're going for a drive.

That's my answer to everything.

Up North. We packed our bags. We did not know when we would come back.

"Which way?"

"North is prettier, I suppose."

My father and I drove. We did not talk. We did not turn on the radio. We ate fast food. Ordering a cheeseburger was excruciating. Everything got extra loud and vivid. The hospital smell still filled my head. Ammonia and sea green. Cashiers grinned and diners chuckled and slurped. Who were these people, chipper and normal? I cried while pumping gas. I pulled onto the shoulder, hit the brakes, and cried some more.

We drove along Lake Huron, where my mom and dad had a sailboat when I was small. They loved to sail. We took weekend cruises along Saginaw Bay until money got tight and they sold the boat and we moved into an apartment. I remember when my mom caught a monster catfish and everybody clapped and took pictures with it. I remember her blushing and giving the catfish away, not wanting to be photographed. My father and I returned to these small port towns. Tawas City. Au Sable. Oscoda. Harrisville. Thunder Bay. He looked at the harbor and remembered past trips while I made phone calls with my eyes shut, leaning against the wall. The body. The death certificate. The cremation. The service. Nobody teaches you how to do these things.

We drove along Lake Superior, crossing into the Upper Peninsula. The Mackinac Bridge gleamed under the full moon, towering cold steel casting long shadows in the deep night. The sign at the Delaware bridge blipped in my head: *If you are in crisis . . .* I couldn't remember the number or I would have called that night. I wanted to keep driving. But we stopped at a cheap motel with fish flies beating against the doors.

I stood in the parking lot and watched my father, sitting on the edge of the bed in his pajamas, munching on a cold slice of sausage and mushroom. My mom was his entire world. I looked up at the stars. I wondered where she was. I remembered a tough biker woman at an AA meeting saying how she only did "foxhole prayers," as if God existed only to get her ass out of a jam. "But that's changing," she said. I sat down. I looked at the sky. I shut my eyes. I waited for a tremor, a signal, or a sign. Nothing came.

We drove to Grand Rapids and I bought a suit on the way.

Guns. I'm helping my father move out of the house and into an apartment. We comb through the clutter of a lifetime. Yearbooks and musty Christmas cards and sentimental vases. We open closets and discover that my mom was a bit of a hoarder. Shoe boxes of receipts from 1986. *Ladies' Home Journals* from the mid-1990s. Stacks of empty notebooks and unsent greeting cards. A mashed clay figurine of my mom that I made when I was six. Trinkets from the days when I felt safe. We don't know what to do with these things.

The house is almost empty. My father has a bag of guns. "You want them? Otherwise I'll take 'em to a pawnshop." A green army duffel leans against the wall with a few shotguns and rifles poking out of the top. My great-great-grandfather's rifle. My grandfather's shotgun. A pistol from World War II. They're beautiful. I pick up a shotgun. Pump action. I know this because I go to the movies.

Handling a gun feels surprisingly natural. Powerful. Like suddenly I'm six again, playing cops and robbers and death is still an abstraction. I peer through the scope.

"What kind of gun is this?" I ask.

"A .22 — I grew up with that gun."

"It feels like a toy."

At night I often dream of guns. Vivid high-pressure fever dreams. I have a recurring dream where I buy a shotgun at a swap meet and immediately lose it under the seat of a rental car. I'm frantically groping for it while attackers crash through the windshield. Sometimes I find the gun in time but the barrel is pointed the wrong way, Wile E. Coyote–style. Or somebody else is pointing a gun at somebody I love. Think fast.

Although they're popular in my dreams, I don't know how I feel about guns. The argument that we're safer if we're armed makes no sense to me. But I remember one night when a pair of swerving high beams flashed in my rearview somewhere in the Sonoron desert. Somebody threw a bottle. I remember wishing I had a gun then.

My father pulls out boxes of X-tra Range Shotgun Shells and Rim Fire Cartridges for the .22. "This ammo is probably still good," he says. He tells me I don't need a permit for rifles and antique pistols. Even if this is true, I don't think driving through the Midtown Tunnel with a trunkful of old guns is a bright idea.

He tells me hunting stories and army stories. My great-great-grandfather feeding his family. My great-grandfather's stint as a night watchman. My grandfather returning from the war. "You can't sell these," I say. I dig the wood. I read the engravings and examine the bullets. I cock the hammers. "Rabbit ears," my father says. "Anyway, I want to get rid of them."

I tell him that we should keep them. I'll take them with me. I'll keep them in storage. We might want them someday.

Ninety-two. My father and I drove across Michigan to visit my mom's mom. My little old Polish grandma that I hardly know. We sit in her living room, a room that has not changed since the late 1960s. Paintings of Jesus hang throughout the house and I dimly remember being terrified of the crucifix at the top of the stairs when I was last here when I was nine or ten. My dad remembers sitting on the same couch in the same place by the window when he first took my mom on a date back in 1974.

These days my grandma keeps the cable news channel cranked to eleven. "For company," she says. Framed photographs of her daughter and her husband sit next to her on the coffee table. Others line the mantle: my mom in kindergarten standing proudly with her classmates after receiving a letter after writing to President-elect Kennedy's daughter, Caroline. My mom and Santa. My mom as a little girl in Catholic school.

"Oh I miss them." My grandmother sniffles and grins, remembering her husband. "We had a little joke, me and him. Whenever he ate ice cream for breakfast or watched too much TV, he'd say to me, 'I'm ninety-two and I can do what I want!' That was his mantra," she says with a shrug. "And who could argue with him? But *I* had to behave. He'd tell me, 'You're only ninety-one. When you turn ninety-two, you can do whatever you want, too.'"

My grandma turned 92 a few weeks after her husband died. "But who am I going to tell?" she says, tears welling up. "He robbed me of my moment."

They were together for sixty years.

My dad and I poked at our coffee cake.

We drive back to Detroit and finished packing up the house. My inheritance was tea. Dozens of boxes of tea. Oolong. Green. Peppermint. Vanilla almond. Mandarin orange. English breakfast. Most of it is decaffeinated because my mom couldn't tolerate caffeine. Darjeeling. Red Zinger. Mountain Berry Ginger. Caramel toffee. The boxes are still sealed and I can picture her at the store, deciding to try something different. To buy herself a treat for a special occasion that never came.

At night I make a cup of tea. After we packed up the house and emptied out the shelves, my dad said I could take the tea or else it was going in the trash. It was too damned sad and he didn't drink tea anyway.

"You're listening to Country Legends AM 690 and that was 'I Want My Old Life Back' . . ."

The Tree that Escaped the Forest. Strange how a particular building or space suddenly becomes an emotional beacon. After my mother's funeral, I drove straight to Bartlesville, Oklahoma. Still wearing my suit, I pointed the rental car south out of Michigan and tore through the Amish fields of Indiana, crossed the Mississippi, and aimed for the Price Tower. Not knowing where else to go, this place called out like a transmitter.

The Price Tower is the perfect place to catch your breath in the middle of America. I first learned about this place several years ago in New Mexico when I stumbled across a magazine article about the tower's renovation as an arts center and hotel. I immediately pointed the car northwest and ripped through deserts and plains. I arrived late at night. The lights were off and the parking lot was deserted, but a handwritten sign was taped to the door: "Welcome Mr. Reeves! Call us for your key."

It was a beautiful room in a strange town in the center of the country and it felt like a secret place. Everything was clean and hushed, like sleeping in a diorama in a forgotten wing of a museum. And so I returned to Bartlesville after the funeral. My fiancée flew from a research project in Malaysia to join me.

At the desk, the clerk looked at the old New York address on my driver's license. "Mott Street, huh? I grew up there. Lived in Chinatown for most of my life. You still there?"

"I'm living in Helsinki now . . . well, I was." Talking was still impossible. "Now I'm . . . living, I don't . . . how did you end up in Oklahoma?"

"Same as you. Life happens. Sign here."

We stayed for a couple of days, trying to make sense of things before she returned to the other side of the world. I took comfort in inviting her to this odd place and showing her the diner where I ate and the quiet streets that I walked when I first drove through Oklahoma three years before.

What does it mean to be a man? Last night I had a terrifying dream. A vivid horrible dream, the sort of dream that drills so deep that you know you'll never talk about it to anybody, and I'm not going to talk about it here. Because I'm too shaken, left with only a couple of flash-bulb images popping in the left corner of my vision and a submerged story line that I can't articulate. And even though I don't believe in dreams or omens or vibrations, I know that my chemistry has permanently shifted somehow. Maybe you've had a dream like this, too.

In this dream, I lost the woman that I love in a horrible way. When I woke up and saw her next to me, I went to pieces. Tears, shaking, the whole shebang. The machinery in my head clicked. I realized that I was put on this earth to make her happy. To protect her no matter what happens, like the hero in a sci-fi movie. Maybe this fearless emotion is what makes somebody a man. Or a father. Or a mother. Or simply a good person. And while I down-shifted from terror to epiphany, she slept soundly with a faint smile on her face.

Ceremony. My mom wanted to be cremated. My father didn't want the ashes. They came in a black plastic cylinder packed in a white cardboard box. I took her ashes with me when I left Detroit.

My mom loved the water. She could watch the waves for hours and I'd wonder what she was thinking about, what held her there for so long. Whenever I called home while traveling, she would say, "Put your toes in the ocean for me." She never saw the Pacific.

I put my mom's ashes into the ocean at Big Sur.

After the funeral mass in Michigan, I pointed the car into the sun and drove for two days straight, twisting up and down the Rocky Mountains, speeding across the floor of the Great Basin, and corkscrewing through Yosemite. Just before dawn, I parked the car along the narrow shoulder of Highway 1, where the edge of the country drops straight down into the crashing ocean. As the sun rose, I scaled down the cliff and opened the black canister and said good-bye.

How do I remember her? As this amazingly protective force. I point the car into the desert and watch the mile markers count down to the Mexican border, and I think about the time when I was six or seven years old and a tornado touched down in a soccer field and she covered me. I mean, she *threw* me to the ground and covered me from the angry wind and noise and dirt. With my mom, there was always this plush sense of being shielded, no matter what happened. I keep looping that scene as I drive south, missing that sensation of being protected from tornados or anything else that came along.

When I was nine, she took to me to the library every day when I was fixated on learning every possible thing about the pyramids in Egypt. I wanted to be an archaeologist. Even back then, she wanted me to be a lawyer. Whenever we'd argue or I'd get excited and prattle on about something, she'd just scrunch up her nose and smile and tell me I was going to make a terrific lawyer. I miss that smile. I speed through the Mojave, wishing I did everything differently. That I held her hand the entire time. That I didn't get so upset when she refused to eat. I'm convinced that it was all a terrible dream and I should probably give her a call.

She died early on a Sunday evening and her death was unexpected. She was a lapsed Catholic and sometimes she cursed in Polish. She called the crusts of bread "bones" and when she was seventeen she studied in France to be a translator. I want you to know a little bit about who she was.

My mom was ridiculously smart. She graduated high school at sixteen and studied at the University of Grenoble in France. She wanted to work for the United Nations and she came very close, and then difficult things happened with her family and she returned home to Grand Rapids, Michigan. Even though she wrestled with panic attacks and agoraphoia all of her life, she never let me see it when I was small. She forced me to do the things that she was scared to do: walk to the store, wait at the bus stop, introduce myself to the neighbors. Only now do I understand how brave this was.

She taught me that the world was big and that I belonged in it.

I pull over in the middle of the Sonoran desert and put on my ugly sneakers. After a few miles, I stop running and think about where to go next.

Somewhere in the Mojave Desert, I get a tattoo.

This is Petr. I first noticed him last week in Monument Valley. Three days later, I spotted him writing in his notebook at a gas station en route to Tuba City. Finally, I flagged him down in the middle of Route 98 in Arizona. He's from the Czech Republic and he's been riding across the country for 58 days now. He started in New York City. "I plan to keep riding until I run out of money," he said.

Although Petr spends many of his nights in a tent, he often enjoys the unsolicited kindness of strangers. A Navajo family took care of him last night and he proudly showed me the road atlas that he received from a concerned couple in Illinois. "I love your country," he said. "The people are so nice." Maybe it was delirium from the 110° sun out there in the red desert, but he looked so happy when he said this that I believed him.

Running into Petr was good for me. Between touring airplane graveyards and driving along the fence lines of strange military installations, it's easy to feel apocalyptic in the desert — and my newfound addiction to talk radio isn't helping. Listening to Petr talk about Chicago, St. Louis, Memphis, and riding alongside the Mississippi reminded me of why I feel so invested in America in the first place: the chaotic rush and cinematic scope of this nation. And this guy is crossing it on his bicycle. I take an odd pride in knowing that Petr's being treated well by strangers in my country.

Development. I drive to the bottom of the country. Pump jacks swing in the sea and refineries shoot fire into the sweaty dark. Old men in wife-beaters play dominoes across folding tables while a parked car cranks the local salsa station. I synchronize my radio.

For twenty-six bucks, I score a cinder-block room in one of those motels with cigarette burns around the sink, a sight that always amazes me. Are people really that busy? The lamp is broken. Bugs zap in the parking lot. I do fifty push-ups and fall asleep slapping mosquitos. In the morning, I wander into town. It's empty. A lot of American towns are empty these days, but the scene in Port Arthur hits me hard. A boom town that was once the home to the largest network of oil refineries in the world, today the downtown is empty.

Aluminum peels. Concrete cumbles. Grass bleeds across the sidewalks into the street. You can see the faded letters from hardware stores and luncheonettes. A dignified town lost to storms, poverty, and systematic neglect. I think about everything I've seen, about all of these photographs and notes of banged-up towns. I'm ready to do something tangible. I want to go beyond computer screens and windshields. I call a law school in New Orleans and make an appointment to visit.

Checkpoint. Driving out of Nogales, I see white lamps and fluorescent steam on the horizon. Flashlights bob in the dark and red taillights glow as the cars ahead of me brake to answer a few questions before zooming back into the night. My engine idles. Gravel crunches under soldier boots. Insects whir in the desert. An officer waves me forward. A big dog strains against a chain leash while the officer puts a flashlight in my face and asks where I'm heading tonight. He wants to know about my job, my hometown, and where my parents live. Another officer sweeps my car with an inspection mirror while I squint and try to remember my lines. Heading to El Paso tonight. Road trip to New Orleans. My dad lives in Michigan. Just a suitcase of clothes in the trunk. A few books on the backseat. Can I go now?

The U.S. Border Patrol operates 33 permanent checkpoints along the southern edge of the country. I was stopped nine times during my drive along the back roads from Calexico to Del Rio. Sometimes it was a "courtesy stop" when I pulled over to take a photograph or catch my breath. Most of the time it was at highway checkpoints like the one in Nogales. Each time I felt amazingly guilty.

The Kindness of Strangers. Low on gas in Louisiana. Scary low. The rental car tells me how many miles are remaining until the tank is empty, which is a cute feature until it starts blinking *16 . . . 15 . . . 14 . . .* and that town I saw on the map in a promising bold typeface turned out to consist of a collapsed barn and an abandoned auto repair shop from the early 1970s. For the first time in years, I talk to God, striking bizarre bargains. *13 . . . 12 . . .* A gas station appears two miles later and now I'm signed up to really quit smoking, go to the gym every day, stop eating fast food, and do something meaningful with my life. But the pump only makes a dry heaving sound.

The kid inside the station runs a pick through his hair and stares at the ceiling. "Sir, we ain't had gas out here for months." In a pretend-calm voice, I explain that I had no idea how empty it was out here and I have exactly eleven miles left until I'm stuck in the middle of it. I'm behaving like an asshole from New York and I apologize for it. He stops looking at the ceiling, laughs, and suddenly he's on the phone, making calls and explaining the situation. "Go six miles east and there's a guy named Mike who runs a garage. You'll get enough gas to get you to Baton Rouge. Hurry now, he's closin' in twenty minutes."

It's late when I reach New Orleans. I love this city, like something dredged from an old familiar dream. Hungry and searching for crawfish, I wander into a crowded bar with a neon sign advertising a 24-hour kitchen. With my road atlas and notebook tucked under my arm, I stand in the doorway, watching the waiters rush and the people laugh and bang the way people do in a noisy tavern. A hand waves and the heavy man attached to it grins. "Over here! Join us, why don'cha?" A beautiful woman at the table smiles and pulls out a chair. He's a painter and she writes corporate training manuals and they've asked me to join them because they think I look like a nice guy. I try my best to play the part.

We swap stories about America. We eat. We talk about the Nevada Test Site, about New York, about the wonders of the interstate system. When you get to talking about America with strangers, it always amazes me how quickly the conversation can assume deep conspiratorial tones. *The problem with this country . . . and if people would only . . . and they need to change how . . . and it's because the government won't tell us . . . and the military . . .* and it always circles back to the mysterious *they.* This is why I take these trips: to put faces, voices, signs, buildings, and towns to *them.*

The conversation drifts toward the war in Iraq and a few political lines are politely drawn across the table. The subject turns to painting. I think it's dead and the painter thinks it's very much alive. Suddenly it's very late and I need to get up early so I can take photographs of more buildings, signs, and people. It does not occur to me to take their picture until two days later when I'm stuck in traffic in Florida.

America. I drive. My rental car drifts past abandoned office buildings and gaping factories. An old man sits on a cardboard box and sings. "I don't care if it gets cold or freezes, just so long as I have my plastic Jesus . . ." I dodge stray shopping carts and dig the swagger of kids in long white t-shirts approaching somebody's passenger side. I think about Detroit and DC and New Orleans and the racism and poverty that rips up this country, forming strange rings, dangerous corners, and dead ends. Other countries don't do this to its citizens. Not like America does. But the rest of the world also skateboards and listens to the blues and lines up to see the latest Hollywood explosion, and I wonder if our dysfunctional and cruel system is required to make all of this product.

Friday night on the Delta: a big man stands near a burning oil drum, throwing wild light against a school bus on blocks that serves as a makeshift bar. The top of the bus is sawed off and people shout and wave and holler as I crunch gravel in the driveway. Friday night in Tribeca: two men drink $85 single malt in a concrete warehouse redone to look like an old factory. Authentic barrels and obscure farming tools sit in the corners.

I speed past gas stations and superstores and housing projects. My rental car scrolls past bleary storefront windows where hardware stores and pharmacies once did business. I give dimes to old men on cardboard boxes and tell myself that I'm a good person. Somewhere in America, there's a spot where Sand Creek Massacre Trail crosses Missile Drive. Maybe it was Idaho. Or Arkansas. I can't remember anymore. Wild-eyed women drive rusted pickup trucks with big dogs hanging out the window. I love the throb and heat of the road. I race through the night and I get greedy — I want to take it all in at once: every bar fight and romance and rusted factory and secret military base.

At a Waffle House in Missouri, I strike up a conversation with a man who has a fantastic mustache. A copy of *How to Make Your First Million in Network Marketing* is tucked under his arm and, before I know it, he jams a business card into my hand and ropes me into a pyramid scheme involving cooling system supplies. Somewhere in the Financial District, a heavy woman in a Starbucks stares at a crinkled postcard of New York's skyline, muttering about Jesus. "And what the fuck is you gonna do, you child of God, you angels, what is you gonna do —" She's wrapped in a rind of dirty blankets and surrounded by a ring of ripped shopping bags. People keep their distance. The baristas gather behind the counter and confer. She does not belong. She pulls a blanket over her head. A sign on the window says *I wish every day was a holiday*. I leave. I run my errands and buy some things and I pass her on the sidewalk a few hours later, surrounded by her bags. I give her a few quarters, feeling complicit.

Imperial. Somewhere south of the Salton Sea and west of the Chocolate Mountains, I saw a cluster of tents and trailers, some with makeshift signs for food and dune buggy repair and outfits like Krazy Karl and the Big Belly Crew. The distant whir of engines cut through the whipping wind. On the horizon, I saw a couple of Rubicon 500s racing across the pink Imperial Dunes. For a moment, I thought I was gazing at the end of the world. Now I'm wondering why I didn't join them.

Rescued. I saw an old bus at the bottom of Texas near Port Isabel, down where it's tropical mayhem and everything is covered in a fine powdery sand. Big white dunes formed big walls along a twisty little road and I caught a glimpse of a bus ripped up with a stuffed animal hanging out of the side. I thought it was gorgeous, so I hit the brakes and hooked a U. I drove my little rental car straight into a sandy ditch. The more I gunned the engine, the deeper I buried the car. Sand sprayed. Pushing, pulling, and cursing didn't help either. The car was stuck. Four different people pulled over to offer help. First, an elderly couple who offered to call somebody. Next, a kid in a football jersey helped me push, but no luck. Then a beefy businessman in a tie threw his sportcoat on the hood and began pushing while I gunned the engine, covering him in sand. He didn't mind. "Just want to get you on your way," he said. "Karma and all." The car didn't budge. He brushed the sand out of his hair and gave me the number for a towing service.

Before I could dial, a monster pickup truck with huge radials, a flaming paint job, and blinding chrome pulled up. Three guys with bandannas and neck tattoos hopped out of the car, conferred in Spanish, and pulled out a massive hook and chain. There was nowhere to attach it under the Hyundair, so I took off my belt and we lashed the chain to the little latch on the trunk. They hit the gas and I pushed. "Man, you wrecked that trunk." That's what a mechanic in Chattanooga said a few weeks later as he whacked at it with a hammer, free of charge.

There's kindness on the road. I found it on lonely strips of highway in Mississippi and New Mexico, on a snowy mountaintop on the Continental Divide, and at the Commodore Perry Service Plaza in Ohio. Strangers gave me gas and helped me down mountains.

American Radio. I catch garbled bits of "Moonlight Serenade" from a distant radio signal while gliding down the streets of Mobile in the pouring rain. Somebody talks about the coming global battle for fresh water. Somebody else says a beloved celebrity might be a cannibal. A woman on the radio says, "I woke up this morning worrying about something I said yesterday. I was kidding around with my students and I used a slang word and they all gasped. I know how sensitive kids are. You create an image with them that is very fragile and I realized that this was a time for prayer."

"That's right. No concern is too small for prayer. Feel the lightness of turning every burden and worry into a prayer —"

Next station.

"— and I'm asking you, what about individual choice? If you're not prepared to accept responsiblity for something as basic as your health, then why not let the government decide *everything* for you? We're only having this discussion because of the great retreat from personal responsibility —"

I change the station. A girl is selling her virginity over the internet to pay for college. A man worries that the government is triangulating his location. A commercial says a few drops of this stuff will make your brain smarter, that you'll feel like you're falling in love all the time. Order now.

And somewhere in the night, a crackling blues record from 1948 plays and Sunnyland Slim sings, "I'm gonna buy me a Johnson machine gun and a carload of explosion balls. And then I'm gonna be a walkin' cyclone baby from Saginaw to Niagara Falls." He says he's going to break his no-good woman out of the penitentiary walls.

American Night. Someday I'm going to live in the Mojave in a double-wide. I'll grow my hair long and buy a ham radio and broadcast into the big American night. For now, I drive to the edges of things. The very bottom tip of Texas or the Florida Keys. Skirting the top rail of Montana or the jumbo forests of the Upper Peninsula. I've traced the Mexican border from Calexico to Del Rio, and I've rushed up to the barbed wire along the edge of the Nevada Test Site. Whenever I hit the edge of something, I squint at the horizon and think, *Up there is New York, and down to the left you've got Los Angeles, and you've got Miami over there.* My favorite moment is when you get in the car and the sun sinks and suddenly it's just you and that yellow line.

If you zoom in, the landscape collapses. Right now people are getting hit by cars and eating salads and writing novels and sitting in prison. Stories crop up everywhere. Slain sheriffs. Faded actresses holed up above dive bars. Odd coincidences, tragic histories, and legal quandaries. I'm obsessing over this country because it's easier to focus on the national than the personal. My addiction to atlases and historical plots is, in part, a refusal to deal with my grief. I know this.

When my mom died and my life unraveled, the road was there for me. I drove for a month, watching the mileage add up and taking strange comfort in the conspiratorial radio, the security checkpoints, the booming loudspeakers at auctions and rallies. As I drove along the Mexican border, I considered pointing the car into the desert and going off the grid for a couple of years; I decided to go to New Orleans instead. I went an awful long way to discover that all of the clichés are true. You love. You lose. You regret. You get scared. You do your best to keep your head together and find something to hang on to.

Appendix

Route

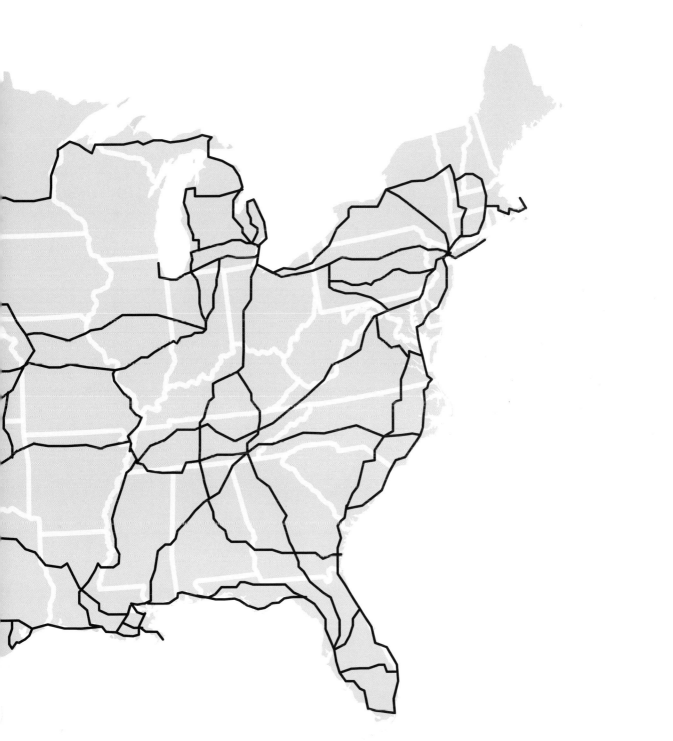

States

Topics

Acknowledgments

Special thanks to my grandfather for answering my questions, to my dad for not asking questions when I borrowed the car, and to Candy Chang for asking lots of questions.

Giant thanks to Austin O'Driscoll at W. W. Norton for knowing what this book was about before I did.

I would also like to thank the people at Dollar Rental Car for not charging me for the busted trunk.

And in no particular order: the Sundown Motel, Grandpa's Country Fried Breakfast at Cracker Barrel, M83, Desert Palms motel, El Cheepo gas stations, the El Governor motor lodge, the Maryland House Service Plaza, the Commodore motel, the Center for Land Use Interpretation, Basic Channel, the Museum of Jurassic Technology, the kid in Colorado who patched my tire on a holiday, Brian Eno, J.G. Ballard, Bohren & Der Club of Gore, the International Delights series of coffee creamers at various gas stations (especially Café con Leche), the innkeepers who let me stay an extra hour or two past checkout, Bob Dylan's "Stuck Inside of Mobile with the Memphis Blues Again," Desert Canyon Inn, Vangelis's "Blade Runner Blues," The Modern Lovers, Coast to Coast AM, Big Red chewing gum, auxiliary audio jacks in rental car stereo systems, unprotected 'default' and 'linksys' wi-fi networks, and the officers in Kentucky, Wyoming, Utah, and Ohio who let me go with a courtesy warning.